Forensic Science in Court

Forensic Science in Court

The Role of the Expert Witness

Wilson Wall
Consultant, Forensic Genetics,
UK

WILEY-BLACKWELL

A John Wiley & Sons, Ltd., Publication

Library of Congress Cataloguing-in-Publication Data

[to come]

ISBN: 978-0-470-98576-2 (hbk)
ISBN: 978-0-470-98577-9 (pbk)

A catalogue record for this book is available from the British Library.

Typeset in 11.25/13.5pt Times by Aptara Inc., New Delhi, India
First Impression   2009

If we sit and think, then we will have made a contribution to philosophy, but not to the sum total of our knowledge and safety, both from individuals and Governments.

Contents

Preface

There are broadly two different methods whereby a court can find the truth of an accusation or in resolving disputes. These two methods are termed inquisitorial and adversarial; they are fundamentally different, but both aim to find the truth in a case. It should always be remembered that with the exception of politically motivated prosecutions, a court will always strive to find the truth of an accusation or dispute. There is a reason for using 'always' twice in that sentence: it is to emphasise that a court wants the truth, as best as can be found, and as a forensic scientist it is your job to help the court come to the correct conclusion. This is, of course, not always easy and so there are miscarriages of justice. Part of the work of a forensic scientist is to provide the court with as much objective evidence as is available to help the court come to the correct conclusion. Forensic evidence can be pivotal for the very simple reason that in some of the most serious crimes, such as rape and murder, there are usually only two individuals present at the time of the assault and it is only the perpetrator and victim who know for certain what happened. Sadly, in the case of murder it is only the assailant who knows for certain and in rape cases the victim may be traumatised and unable to be sure of an identification.

When the inquisitorial procedure is used, the tribunal looks for the facts in the case directly and is able to call witnesses in its own right and decides, without necessarily consulting with the various parties involved, what needs to be known to come to a conclusion in the case. The individuals or groups involved in the dispute would normally attend the inquisitorial hearing and are usually given a chance to put their side of events, but control of the investigation stays exclusively with the investigating individual or tribunal. Although it is often thought that an impartial investigator can use the inquisitorial method to dig out the truth of a case rapidly, the converse is a disadvantage of the system; it is always possible that the investigator may not be disinterested, which would result in a prejudicial result, with the possibility that the aggrieved party may not feel they have been given adequate time to make their point.

In the United Kingdom inquisitorial hearings tend to be confined to such tribunals as planning applications and Coroners' Courts, where the coroner will call what witnesses are thought necessary; it is not the right of the interested parties to call witnesses, although they may with the leave of the court. All other hearings are adversarial. In other countries, as in the case of most of Europe, the inquisitorial system is the norm for hearings.

Civil law, as a description of a legal system, refers to a system of law which is based on a modified system of law used in ancient Rome. Civil law in Rome was based partly on legislation and partly on opinions brought forth by legal scholars. The eventual result was described as the Body of Civil Law, *Corpus Juris Civilis*. This is sometimes referred to as the Justinian Code, having been instigated by Emperor Justinian. After the adaptation and adoption of ancient civil law by France, civil law spread throughout the French colonies and possessions.

In contrast to the inquisitorial system of finding the truth, in the UK the system is adversarial. This revolves around the idea that the two parties in either a civil dispute, or criminal proceedings, argue their case, with an eventual winner. The presiding judge or tribunal does not generally intervene, but allows each side to put their case as they see fit within the rules of engagement, the rules of procedure. Unlike the inquisitorial system, the adversaries are directly responsible for calling witnesses for their side of the argument, but they are allowed to question witnesses called by the opposing party. As a consequence of this system it is supposed that every scrap of evidence will be revealed. Unfortunately the truth can sometimes come off second best in this system, although that is not to say that overall it is either better or worse than the inquisitorial system. In some ways adversarial systems are dependent on the oratorical ability of the combatants. As you will note from the language – adversarial, combatants, rules of engagement – the court can be quite an aggressive place in this system. It is a method used extensively in countries which practise a common law system.

Common law refers to the laws, often unwritten, which have developed over the centuries, and are based on common customs within the country. Just as civil law spread through the French colonies, so common law as a system of implementing justice spread through the colonies of the UK. Within this system the law is broadly based upon precedents created by the judiciary. This gives it great flexibility when dealing with a changing society, so within prescribed limits a judge may depart from previous precedents and create a new one. Because of this immense flexibility resulting in precedents being created in all manner of ways, common law is not collated in a single place and consequently is described as unwritten law. It is of course written down, but in such disparate places as court reports and newspaper reports of cases.

One of the fundamental differences between inquisitorial and adversarial systems is that in the latter the judge instructs the jury, which then comes to a verdict by deciding on the facts that are relevant. Even within this system there are times when a judge, or panel of judges, will decide both the law and the facts that are relevant; these are nearly always civil actions.

Interestingly, in the USA the basis of the American legal system was the common law at the time of the War of Independence. This has evolved into a rather different style of justice, but broadly fits into the general form of common law. In the USA there is one state, Louisiana, which pursues a court system based on civil law, due primarily to Louisiana having been for much of its formative years a French enclave.

In this book, the bulk of the descriptions of the work of the forensic scientist will revolve around the adversarial system as it is found in the UK, but the general descriptions of standards, activities and interpretation of results are universal. It should be axiomatic for all scientists that what is true in one country is true in all countries. I have worked in many countries as an expert witness: the structure of the judicial system should not affect the work of the forensic scientist; objective reporting of the results will be the same everywhere, but;hat the court makes of it may not be. It cannot be emphasised enough that forensic evidence should never be partisan, because that way leads to corruption and eventually a discrediting of all evidence. Mistakes do happen, but as long as the mistakes are genuine mistakes and not perversions of justice, the system can cope with such hiccups; what it cannot deal with is dishonesty, or an attitude which says 'that will do'.

1

Where The Law Comes From: You Don't Mess About With The People

It is very easy to disparage the rule of law, but as a forensic scientist you need to know two things. The first is that it does rule; the times of arbitrary rules come and go. We always seem to come to the same conclusions as despots come and go – that the rule of law is the most important glue that sticks a society together. The second is that a forensic scientist has a duty to their subject and the people they serve – this does not mean the payers of wages, or even the formulators of laws, but society and truth.

It is generally thought that the English legal system and therefore the legal system extant throughout the old colonies and the Commonwealth originated in Greek and Roman law. The situation is a little more complicated than that, but this is what we shall explore.

It is important to realise that laws, real laws, have a sound philosophical basis. There are many accounts of the origins of the rule of law, common law. It can be said in the West that our ideas of law stem quite clearly from ancient European philosophies. During the fifth century BC Athens was at its height of power and was also a political system directly ruled by the citizenship. Indeed, the now widely used and understood word *Candidate* refers to the citizens of Athens who were eligible and canvassing to become senators – they

Forensic Science in Court: The Role of the Expert Witness   Wilson Wall
© 2009 W. J. Wall

wore white. The other time you may have seen this use of the Greek derivation is *Candida albicans*, referring to the white discharge caused by that fungal infection.

This association between the Greek heritage and modern European usage even extends to our word Police. This is from *Polis*. Now, in modern terms it means exactly what you understand it to do. But in Greek and some other regimes it was the political community, even the body politic, and elsewhere this has been transformed into the *Politbureau*, which was a political instrument, not necessarily for the good.

So what we see in Athens over 2000 years ago was a system where any male citizen, of any age or status, could sit as a magistrate, juror or on the governing council. There was no system or set of individuals who ran the law, so equality was a fundamental part of the way in which the law was handled and administered. This, as we shall see, is the way in which the common law has developed and evolved in the United Kingdom but with some surprising twists and turns for the forensic scientist.

What has happened so often with discussions of the history of law is that it can become a little bogged down, not in detail but in philosophical points. This is not what we need to know. What we need to know is who wrote what and when and also why? Unfortunately the growth of the law is as complicated as the growth of an organism and just as convoluted. In the Greek system, although there was great pride in the state being a true democracy run directly by the citizenry, it was not an egalitarian society. Certain groups were treated differently from each other, the second class being primarily children, slaves, non-citizens and women. It was also true that any male citizen over the age of 30 could become a paid juror or a magistrate. Where equality did reign was in the application of the law *within* any given group. As you can readily imagine, such a system might easily be corrupted. To guard against this the law was set apart from the legislature, a situation now routinely held to in enlightened secular societies. Consequently the courts are there to interpret and respect the law while maintaining its integrity, they are not there to make law arbitrarily. This does sometimes appear odd when apparently strange happenings are reported in the press, for example when a rape victim is put through the ordeal of being cross-examined by the accused. The judge cannot stop this because it is the law that an accused can confront their accuser and carry out such a cross-examination if they so wish, even if the result is repugnant to all those present.

As time moved on and Athens lost power, but not wealth, three very clear-thinking philosophers emerged. Socrates, who was condemned to death by the democratic process, taught Plato, who taught Aristotle. These three produced seminal works on ethics and law. For the curious these books are always available, but I must say quite hard going as they focus on law as a philosophy. They do, however, have very important things to say which resonate today as true and valuable. For the reason that after 2000 years their words still seem to be valuable guides, it is worth just contemplating what the main drive of their collective thesis was.

In broad terms, and briefly, law was seen as transcending changes in fortunes within a state or country; it was seen as immutable and based on some fundamental principles which could not be changed. This is particularly interesting because it is easy to think of laws as simple instructions such as 'do not cross the road when the light is red'. But this misses the point. This injunction is a simple instruction, but has an immutable principle behind it, which is to cooperate with your fellow citizens. Plato insisted that government should be subject to the law, indeed held accountable to it, not the other way around. This inevitably makes for a slow and turgid legislature, but also one which, generally, upholds the values of the individual. Aristotle added a significant item to this when he insisted that law should essentially be a product of reason, not of passion, or, as we would probably say in the twenty-first century, a 'knee-jerk' reaction. When Plato and Aristotle were working, thinking and contemplating, they came to a conclusion which none would dispute, could possibly dispute, except the tyrant and self-deluding dictator – that is, that The Law is there to further the good of the community and enhance the moral virtue of the citizenry. This is most obviously epitomised in every legal system which is written down: murder is forbidden. There are, in fact, few rights which are regarded as absolute, rather than those bestowed by government or custom, but not being maliciously killed is one of them.

It all comes down to what is just is lawful and fair; this is the position of both Plato and Aristotle. Realistically this cannot be gainsaid, otherwise you are a dictator.

So after the Athenian system and decline of Greek power there arose a new force – the Romans. They, too, had an influence down the ages on the way in which law has been expressed. Cicero wrote much along the same lines as Plato and Aristotle that a republic may have a king, but the king must abide by the law, the same as every citizen. Broadly, Cicero held all that was Athenian to be true regarding the law, though not when it came to political thought regarding government. It is unfortunate that what transpired within Roman law was a shift away from what we would now regard as true and fair into an arbitrary system of law. This was epitomised by the Justinian edict within written statutes that the prince is not bound by the laws (for prince, here, read emperor).

With the decline in Greek and Roman influence on the history of Northern Europe a strange and interesting change took place. This was primarily a development of a concept that had been written down in ancient Greece – that laws stood even when rulers fell. Even so, there was always the possibility for tyranny and this did happen.

There is a period which for convenience sake we tend to describe as the Middle Ages. This is for no sensible reason other than the whim of historians. It is usually said to have started about the fifth century and ran for a thousand years, until the Renaissance. The fifth century was about the time that the Roman Empire collapsed, and here is an interesting aside. It has been suggested, quite seriously, that while the Greeks and Romans were very good at fundamental thought, such as Euclidean geometry and philosophy, they used old technology. Yes, it was good, but it was also just a refinement of technology that had been used for centuries; it was not innovative. The ability to build a bridge of unsurpassed strength was well known, but only of short spans, for example. Had they ventured to look at the application of their science, new materials, better materials, would undoubtedly have been the result and with that the development of a unified Europe a thousand years earlier than it took to achieve. But they were essentially tribal and while sophisticated they were also brutal; the result was the 'collapse of stout party', in this case the Romans.

So, we have the Middle Ages, with the first few centuries described as the Dark Ages. This was marked by wars and invasions from the east and Germanic tribes. I will not go into the history, that is for you to do if you are interested, but it is worth noting that some of these tribes have left us with words which now epitomise negative aspects of civilisation. So we have the Huns from the east and then the Goths, Visigoths and Vandals from Central Europe. They were all acting against an historical oppression without thought. The devastation of Rome did not have any positive result and when the followers of Mohammed decimated North Africa and southern Spain and France, the trade and contact between civilisations slowed down. At the same time the Vikings were working their way south. This is also quite interesting, in that in the UK a number of words and names have been incorporated into the language. A good example is the surname Vara, or Varo, which appears on the east coast of England; this is a name of Viking origin and quite distinct from such names as Smith and Archer which are Anglo-Saxon.

To return to how the law evolved, with the collapse of the unified Europe of the first millennium, small systems of law arose, based upon a rule of nothing more than bullying. This took the form of not just physical manipulation of the population but also taking advantage of the financial and social collapse of the Roman Empire. The general way in which it worked was that during the ninth and tenth centuries despots arose who usurped power from the citizenry. This was done by controlling land and labour by force; if you control then you rule, *ipso facto* you make the law. This was not a happy position to be in if you were on the receiving end of a dictator. Let's make it clear that during this period of European development there were a lot of petty dictators who ruled by their own set of rules; Socrates, Plato and Aristotle might never have existed, but the principles still existed. It is almost a solipsism that if Socrates, Plato and Aristotle had not existed, somebody would have come to the same conclusion – that there are things an individual or state cannot do to another member of society with impunity, that is to be a tyrant or bully.

Although this feudal system did put virtually absolute power into the hands of a small number of land-owning gentry, lords and their vassals over the serfs under their control, there was also an element of the lords serving the serfs. So the rulers would intervene in disputes and make judgments and also offer protection to their serfs against marauding groups of thieves as well as providing for them during times of hardship. This made a lot of sense, for while the serfs were under the power of the lord and his vassals it was implicitly recognised that without this workforce on the land and being able to raise armed forces in times of strife, the lord was an empty vessel. In this system the Church played an increasingly important part – as lords with huge amounts of land. This was often achieved by bequests and resulted in some of the larger bishoprics having a bishop who was effectively a baron.

Throughout the Middle Ages the only presence which spanned the whole of Western Europe was the Catholic Church. This entire medieval period was essentially mud and marble: mud for the serfs and marble for the lords. It was a time simply of survival, of utility without the scope for improvement. During this period, around the thirteenth century, a book was produced which has resonated down the years and is well worth reading, in translation from Latin, that is *Summa Theologia* written by Thomas Aquinas. He resurrected the thoughts of Aristotle regarding the law. It was this influence that the Catholic Church played upon as virtually every individual in medieval Europe was a Catholic, including kings and princes, and was deemed therefore to owe fealty to the Pope, who claims direct succession from St Peter. This was about as unifying as Europe got for a long time, but it did mean that there was a certain amount of unity in the law, though, it has to be said, not a great deal.

During this period there developed a system called customary law. This is particularly interesting because it held that kings were under the law, even though customary law was not generally written down but claimed to an ancient heritage, which in times of short and brutal lives was important. Even when these laws were written down they were seen not as new laws but as codifying existing ancient laws. During this period an uneasy situation began to settle upon the law givers with the dawning realisation that without ever-increasing lands and serfs there has to be a truce, of sorts, which means that the law should stand for everyone, with no exceptions. It was essentially this idea which resulted in a most famous document being produced, namely Magna Carta. It was produced and signed in 1215, about 10 years before Thomas Aquinas was born, and heralded a distinct change in attitude to the law. In that it is very significant; in the detail of its content it is far less so.

We need to go back a little in time to put this document into context, before we look at the relevant detail for the law of today.

By 1199 England had become a powerful state run by a monarch, and this state included parts of what is now France. The inability of King John to defend his holdings in France meant that there was considerable pressure to raise revenue to cover the costs of his defence. This led to extortionate taxes, and remember that while this was the king's prerogative, lords, barons and free men could hold the king accountable. So when the activities of the king became arbitrary and potentially extreme, a group of barons did something which was unprecedented – they held the king accountable for his actions.

Although we think that Magna Carta is somehow pivotal in the democratic rule of law, it was really a signed statement of 'sorry, I won't do it again' from the king to his barons. There was very little in it for the populace.

Magna Carta is Latin and means literally Great Charter. The text is written in Latin. This is of interest because, while illiteracy was widespread among the general population, the only common language among the groups that held power was Latin; they could read it, but not always talk in it. There were so

many different languages among the people that the best *lingua franca* for
written communication was Latin.

Magna Carta was signed at Runnymede. We know this because at the bottom of the document the last section runs 'Given by our hand in the meadow
that is called Runnymeade, between Windsor and Staines, on the fifteenth day
of June in the Seventeenth year of our reign.' That was 1215. The run-up
to this momentous event started long before 1215 with King John unable to
defend what would now be seen as overseas holdings, which led to extortionate tax demands and reprisals against defaulters. Further, it was thought that
his administration of justice was quirky and unreliable. Against this backdrop
a group of barons demanded a charter of liberties against the behaviour of
the king. This was early in the year, but nothing happened and so they took
up arms and captured London in May of that year. Negotiations started on
10 June and finally produced the 'Articles of the Barons', the Great Seal was
attached and the situation went back to normal. Then, after the document was
signed and sealed it was taken to the Chancery and formalised into what we
now know as Magna Carta (it is not normally prefixed by 'the'). The Chancery
not only produced a formal document, but also made copies. The exact number is unknown, but it is said that they were distributed to bishops, sheriffs and
some other worthies, so there must have been quite a few. However many there
were, we do know that four of the original edition survived. It is now unlikely
that there are any more copies remaining undiscovered, but you never can tell.
During the copying process, changes were made. We know this because each
of the surviving four are all slightly different in small ways, in size, shape and
text, with what appears to be last-minute revisions at the foot of one document
being incorporated into the body of the text of another one.

The influence of Magna Carta is considerable, even to the US Constitution
and Bill of Rights, but it should also be remembered that Magna Carta was
reissued after the death of King John in 1216 and again by Henry III, the tendency being for the charter to be gradually shortened. Although in translation
it is usual to divide Magna Carta into paragraphs, it was actually written as
solid text with no breaks. Before moving on to the areas which directly im-
pinge on forensic science, there were a number of very precise clauses which
are worth a mention, such as 'no widow shall be compelled to marry', 'all fish
weirs shall be removed from the Thames' and 'there shall be a standard width
of dyed cloth, russet and haberject, namely two ells within the selvedge'. At
that time standard units were not very common, so all we can say is that an ell

was about 45 inches in England and 37 inches in Scotland, or about 114 cm and 94 cm respectively.

Although Magna Carta started a movement and trend towards the rights of individuals not to be interfered with by an uncontrolled monarch or dictator, there are very few parts of the Great Charter which are still in force today. One is supposed to guarantee the freedom of the Church in England. While this is generally true, it should be remembered that Henry VIII not only closed many monasteries down, but changed what was a Catholic Church into the Church of England. There is also a section which states that the City of London shall retain all its ancient liberties, along with all other cities, boroughs, towns and ports, which shall enjoy their own liberties and freedoms. This indicated that the City of London was regarded as a special place. The only other remaining clause is the one which is of greatest significance to the individual and especially anyone dealing with matters forensic. Simply put in translation:

> No free man shall be seized or imprisoned, or stripped of his rights or possessions, or outlawed or exiled, or deprived of his standing in any other way, nor will we proceed with force against him, or send others to do so, except by the lawful judgement of his equals or by the law of the land. To no one will we sell, to no one deny or delay right or justice.

So there it stands, no imprisonment without trial and no corruption in the system.

Because some of the charter's contents are associated with righting specific wrongs, with individuals being named, the charter was occasionally updated and reissued.

For centuries Magna Carta held a position of influence on the law. This was not to everyone's liking and the level of influence waxed and waned through the centuries. A big change occurred in 1828 when the first Offences Against the Person Act was passed by Parliament and in so doing repealed a clause of the charter. The significance of this event was that until that time, whatever personal feelings were involved, the popular concept was that it was an inviolable base upon which the law stood. Once this hurdle had been cleared it was a relatively short period of a century and a half before all but the parts remaining today were repealed.

This document had one other effect, of a form which is in a way surprising, since it inspired the production of the first attempt to review the whole of English law. The significance of this is that until this time the law was, essentially, piecemeal. The man involved was probably Henry de Bracton, his work now being referred to as simply 'Bracton', but it is also true that he was from the West Country in England and that names were rather more fluid than we consider them today, so he was probably named Bratton originally. Although his early years remain temporally distant and vague, we do know that when he died he was buried in the nave of Exeter Cathedral in 1268. Besides taking assizes he was also variously rector of several places, including, in 1262, Barnstaple in Devon. Later he became Archdeacon there and eventually Chancellor of Exeter Cathedral. This is of interest because at this time it was common for senior figures in most professions to be ecclesiastically trained as well. Indeed, well into the nineteenth century it was normal to be qualified in matters clerical as well as your chosen subject if you wanted to be a lecturer at one of the older universities in England.

Now, what Bracton did was remarkable. He seems to have started as a justice in 1245, not so long after the signing of Magna Carta, and then carried on until his death. Most of his judicial work seems to have been in the south-west of England – Cornwall, Devon and the like. What brings him to notice here is his work *Bracton on the Laws and Customs of England*. This was the first attempt to make sense out of a rather ragged system of laws. It was written in Latin, as so much was at the time, remembering that when I say written in Latin, I do mean written by hand in Latin. There was no printed work in England until the fifteenth century. But even after 300 years Bracton's work was so important that it made it into print, the first edition being produced in 1569. It was still in Latin and remained so until a translation was produced between 1878 and 1883, but still with accompanying Latin text. Even during the thirteenth century an attempt was made to expand the influence of Bracton by translating it into French, the reason being that the nature of the document was based on Roman law, as were most systems in Europe at that time. It is easy to forget that the printing press using movable type was not found in Europe until Johannes Gutenberg invented it between 1436 and 1440. Printing was used in China long before that, but in a different way. Gutenberg's first project was an obvious choice for a deeply religious period – the Bible. England was not far behind with Caxton starting to print books at Westminster in 1476, the first being produced in 1477. A year later printing was underway in Oxford, which eventually through twists and turns over a hundred years gave rise to Oxford University Press.

The period during which Bracton was producing his work was a turbulent time in England and it would seem that while Bracton tried to codify the laws that were in place he was ultimately thwarted by having been asked to return some of the material which he had used as primary sources for his treatise, so it was unfinished and possibly not entirely his own work. Nonetheless it stands out as a seminal work of English law. Interestingly, one of the more arcane areas which he discussed was associated with money lending and debt. This was a big topic at the time because there simply was not a huge amount of coinage in circulation and certainly no banknotes. So although a baron may be a wealthy man, it was in terms of land and property rather than cash. Consequently, when relatively large amounts of cash were needed it was necessary to borrow it; this even went as far as the king. So money lending was, as now, important and the regulation of the process necessary.

It is of interest that paper money was in circulation in or around 960 in China, the Song dynasty, but did not appear in Europe until Stockholm Banco produced it in 1660. In England it was 1694 before paper money appeared. For many years it remained as promissory notes, 'I promise to pay the bearer on demand the sum of one pound', the piece of paper representing the money. Now, of course, the piece of paper *is* the money.

Bracton goes into some considerable detail regarding the almost philosophical aspects of this regulation, starting with the borrowing of money or goods by one person from another. This process, the borrowing and repayment, was settled without forensic evidence by the testing of oaths, compurgation. The borrower swears they either did not borrow the money, or that it was repaid. The borrower's neighbours do likewise and so, if the borrower is more plausible than the lender, the person said to have done the borrowing walks away without the debt, but like so many such cases there are really only two people who know the truth, the lender and the borrower, now the alleged borrower. This, as can be imagined, was an area in which there was inevitably going to be ill feeling whoever won and this would often be directed at the court as well. In more serious cases, those which might involve physical violence for example, at the beginning of the thirteenth century an outcome could be arrived at either by battle or trial by ordeal. Ordeals came to a relatively abrupt end in 1215 with the publication of a Papal Canon forbidding the involvement of priests in trials by ordeal. Until then it was customary for a priest to be employed to encourage the fire or water to distinguish between the guilty and innocent. So of three potential methods of determining guilt or innocence, that is battle, testing of oaths (called at that time compurgation) and ordeal, one was now no longer available. This led to a rather unusual state in that the accused, languishing in jail, still had to choose to be held to account by a jury, rather than have their oath put to a divine test. This resulted in a lot of space being taken up in prison by individuals who did not make such a decision. Beyond that it remains largely unknown as to what lengths the proceedings in court went to find the truth. What we do know is that courts were largely local affairs, counsel for the defence virtually unknown and verdicts simply stated in the plea roll as guilty or not guilty. So it is quite likely that without direction, not only were the courts local affairs, but so too the administration and interpretation of justice.

When the judge was asked to direct the jury on an issue that was of particular significance or difficulty, it would not have been unusual for the case to stop while the judge acquired information and insight from colleagues in London. Even under these circumstances it would have been quite normal for the debating lawyers in London to take their initiative from the opinions and attitudes of laymen. It should be remembered that the rule of law is not applied to society – that way lays tyranny – it is constructed out of the minds of those at whom it is aimed, and so constructed that the constructor accepts it as ruling them as well as everyone else. This even extends to the monarch. It was the introduction of jury trials in a more widespread manner that started to upset the rising merchant classes. Swearing an oath for a religious individual is an activity not to done without certainty; if you believe in a literal heaven and hell, damnation becomes a reality. The merchants were not happy with the erosion of oath-swearing because their entire basis of activity was honesty and trust, and their word was the only assurance they considered necessary for a deal to be struck. In a way this was rather odd, because what they were doing was breaking a stranglehold which had been the basis of society from its very beginning – feudalism.

The feudal system more or less gave landowners rights over individuals who worked for them, but by the end of the thirteenth century this had changed beyond recognition; changes continued long after, but the seeds were sown. In a feudal system the nobility have status, power and wealth, but the wealth is in land and production. The rising merchant classes, so despised by the Church for their base use of commerce, were wealthy in what we would think of as a modern way – they had money, probably no land, although that was always seen as a status thing, and financial leverage which the nobility lusted after.

The merchants were therefore no longer controllable in a feudal system and the merchant laws, set up by merchants and for merchants, ended up as part of the broad body of common law. The nobles were a bit hacked off about this, but that is evolution and evolution is what the law was going through.

So what we have at this point is a muddle – a muddle because different groups are dispensing justice based upon different ideas. There is no written constitution to fall back upon, only the unwritten one based on documents such as Magna Carta and the Act of Habeas Corpus, among others. The process of developing the law was slow, but that is why it has a solidity and can be easily transported from place to place. This is also why violations of human rights and war crimes can actually be put to trial, because there is a moral right for every individual to stand up and say when there has been a wrong committed, or when they do not agree with the outcome of a case. In the case of human rights the problem may creep up on the forensic scientist. Consider this: that the law is based upon a robust concept of *fairness*, natural law, the idea that you can say that something put upon you is unfair. That is reasonable; you may not be able to articulate exactly why it is unfair, but you know that it is. So what happens when you know, as a forensic scientist, that the outcome of a court case is wrong? You stand up and shout – that is your duty to the law and, more importantly, to society.

As time went on the rule of law became pre-eminent and was based on the notion, somewhat arbitrarily, that the people governed by the laws not only must agree to them, but in so doing in some way wrote them. It was in this context that philosophical arguments arose about the nature of the rule of law and the structure of society. This was a period which effectively returned to the questions asked in Rome and Greece centuries earlier. Now the philosophers were notables such as John Locke, Thomas Hobbes and David Hume. The arguments were legion and well rehearsed so that a remarkable thing happened in the English legal system. Although for centuries, more or less until we joined the European Union, there was no written constitution, there was also no written statement of the rights of an individual. The common law was supposedly the product of gradual evolution of ideas through time. The common law rules for the majority of offences and misdemeanours applied to all citizens equally, whether they were private individuals or civil servants. So although there was not a document in the same sense as the US Constitution, there was an unwritten constitution based on various documents, such as Magna Carta and some of the more robust pieces of legislation which determined the length of a Parliament and the relationship between monarch and Parliament.

All this meant that modernisation of the law, the power of rule, came much earlier to England than elsewhere in Europe. It was a situation where the rule of law was essentially centralised, but carried out locally. In contrast, it was common for local systems of rules and regulations to be used on mainland Europe and even when there was a central process of appeals it would be usual for the appeal to be heard in the context of local customs and governance – more like a teacher holding sway than a headmaster stating an absolute truth. Not that they do, but you get the idea.

During the period from when Bracton was produced to the nineteenth century there were many things which occurred to change laws and cause what could have become major upsets had the rules been strictly applied. One such is the idea that it was mandatory for adults to undergo archery practice. This was indeed the case during the reign of Henry VIII, but the 'State Law Revision Act' of 1863 stopped all of that, and further clear-ups took place with the Betting and Gaming Act of 1960 which removed many such arcane rules and regulations. The development of English law has many such tales to tell and they should not be dismissed lightly. While many states may pride themselves upon a constitution, it was the gradual development of the centralised rule of law which gave the English system such robustness and flexibility. The most obvious problem comes from cases such as the USA where there is a constitutional 'right' to bear arms (remember that everyone has the right to bare arms). Because it is written into the constitution it becomes very difficult to alter it – even when common sense declares that it is no longer appropriate to have a gun and the availability of weaponry capable of high-speed destruction is available, when it was not at the time of the constitution being written.

But let us go backwards a little. Reform of the criminal law took place in and around 1830, but prior to that, although the concept of fairness had been employed, what had not been valued was what Gilbert and Sullivan would describe as 'let the punishment fit the crime':

> My object all sublime
> I shall achieve in time –
> To let the punishment fit the crime –
> The Punishment fit the crime
> —*1885 Mikado Act II*

Two notable features of punishment stand out: the first is transportation and the second is capital punishment. Let us look at capital punishment first. It started out as a condemnation of the soul, so the more brutal and humiliating against the religious beliefs of the individual, the better. This was not for the benefit of the condemned, but to deter others and make the family aware of the heinous crime that was committed. Sadly it was generally little more than ritual murder in itself, of no value and with no place in a civilised society.

During the early eighteenth century, in England there were approximately 200 crimes for which you could be sentenced to death. Now, no matter what your personal philosophy is regarding institutionalised death, I maintain that it is unlikely that you could genuinely come up with even a quarter of that number of legal transgressions for which you could justify killing someone. During the whole eighteenth century there was another factor which became involved in the administration of justice. This was fear. Remember that guilt or innocence is separate from sentencing, so what we find during this period with minor crimes being given the death penalty is that there had to be a gradation in the severity of that penalty. Today we would describe it as cruel and unusual punishment, or torture, but then it was the deliberate installation of fear. So in 1752 there was a trend towards instant execution upon conviction, at least within two days, which rendered the possibility of an appeal hopeless. At the same time the prisoner was held in solitary confinement on bread and water. So there was no possibility of appeal, comfort or saying goodbye to your family. It was also deemed necessary that the guilty party should suffer in both this world and the next, hence the installation of fear.

Just so that you are aware of how inhuman the law could be, and remember just how much has happened on every continent in the world since 1700 England, let us have a look at what went on then, compared with now. But also remember that some things which you, as a forensic scientist, will be asked to investigate will appear medieval, and not all political regimes are straightforward and honest. You always report what you find, not what someone else would like you to find.

The fear, mentioned above, was based on the idea that since relatively minor offences could carry the ultimate penalty, such as vagrancy in soldiers and sailors, letter stealing and sacrilege, it was deemed necessary to create a punishment which was even more severe for more horrific crimes. This was obviously difficult, but the ingenuity of Parliament was up to the task, with further terrors for the criminal. This consisted of the body being handed over for dissection, or the body was to be hung in chains and all the convict's lands and goods were to be forfeit. It was this which struck the most fear into the convict. Women could be dissected, but not hung in chains. It did, in fact, become worse for some crimes, because of the nature of the execution. Some of these crimes were coining, that is counterfeiting, or petty treason, that is the murder of a lord by a vassal, or a husband by his wife. In the case of a woman the sentence was that she would be, originally, dragged through the streets, but later in a cart, and then burnt until she was dead. Although strictly against the rules of interference, the executioner was often instrumental in shortening the suffering by strangling the individual first. This brutal method of death, put your hand in a flame and then consider the outcome of progressive immolation, was changed in 1790 to hanging instead; the last burning was carried out in 1789.

The number and severity of conditions under which death was the penalty slowly decreased until by 1957 there were only five clear charges which carried the possibility of death. These were two murders committed on different occasions, murder in the course of a theft, by shooting or causing an explosion, resisting arrest or during an escape, or murdering a police or prison officer. Finally, in 1969, Parliament abolished capital punishment for murder. The thing to remember about this is that while you can restore freedom to an innocent individual, you cannot restore life to one. Unfortunately, it is without doubt true that miscarriages of justice have taken place which resulted in a person's execution; it is also true that a person might be guilty of the offence as charged, but should that result in their execution if it was a case of trivial larceny?

An alternative to the death penalty was transportation. Now, this is often thought of as transportation to Australia, but this is not how it started. Transportation to the Caribbean colonies was also a common mode of punishment. It was during the late eighteenth century and early nineteenth century that transportation was at its height, at least as a sentence. Many of those sentenced to transportation had the sentence reduced to a rather more minor punishment, or were not transported at all. With the American War of Independence in 1776 it became impossible to transport convicts to the Americas, so Australia became the destination of choice, except, of course, with the convicts themselves. It was the Transportation Act of 1718 that codified the process of transportation. The reason for this was not, as is sometimes reported, that it provided cheap labour for the growing colonies, which it did, it was more about trying to eradicate the criminal element at home. Other punishments just did not seem able to stem the tide of criminal activity and so for offences which were not capital, or where a capital offence had been pardoned, it was normal for transportation to be substituted. This was generally 7 years for a non-capital offence and 14 years for a commuted capital crime. Returning from transportation before the term of the sentence was completed would result in hanging. This was a rare event simply because it would be hard enough to find a passage and make your way home – the possibility of being identified afterwards was remote.

It did not take long after 1718 for transportation to be seen by the judiciary as a very expedient method of getting rid of both first-time offenders and recidivists. At this point, what had previously been short and sharp penalties turned into transportation, for approximately 50% of acts of thievery. So between 1718 and 1776 it was a common form of punishment to transport convicts to the American colonies. This was suddenly curtailed in 1776 and the problem of what to do with the convicted started to be come a problem on a massive scale. The prisons were full of prisoners sentenced to transportation, but with nowhere to send them. Many of them ended up on floating hulks on the Thames in London and in the harbour at Portsmouth on the south coast. The outcome of this was that the government of the day decided that the armed forces were the best place for these individuals; some were pardoned and some were deemed to have served an adequate sentence and were therefore released back into an unsuspecting society.

After the end of the war in the American colonies it was assumed, incorrectly, that transportation would resume, but of course it did not – the newly independent states were not about to start taking what was seen as the social dregs of England. What was to be done? The realisation dawned that Australia had potential, even if it was further away, and also needed cheap labour. In this period it was still seen as legitimate to control, or try to control, criminal activity by the use of fear. There is no doubt that transported individuals suffered greatly, both in their passage and upon landfall, but transportation was not always recognised as that, being seen as an excuse by the authorities to imprison individuals in conditions of hard labour for the duration of their sentence, a much longer period than would have been suffered in England.

A problem, not foreseen by politicians, was that after the Napoleonic wars there was a huge increase in demobilised servicemen with no money and no jobs, so by 1815 crime was on the increase again. Consequently transportations started to increase as a standard part of the panoply of punishments. This went on for some considerable time until a change took place in Parliament which meant that laws were rather more enlightened. Laws expressly for the benefit of the landed or moneyed were gradually being reduced in favour of a softer, more concerned regime. There would, however, be considerable time between 1850 and the point when it was clearly understood that Parliament and the social order were at the will of the people and not just monarchs and lords. When transportation effectively ceased in 1863 there were people born who would be alive and kicking in the First World War, and for many of them would be senior policy makers. This caused a change in policy that lasted throughout the twentieth century. It may or may not have been motivated by the problems of the 1850s, but what is certain is that a mixture of technology and politics resulted in the Defence of the Realm Act (DORA). We have seen that government had recognised that it was essentially running the country for the population, rather than itself, but there was also an increasing realisation that at times of war in the twentieth century ordinary measures would not necessarily be enough to protect the nation. During the early weeks of the First World War, in fact on 8 August 1914, DORA was introduced to the country; it was short and was quickly superseded by the Defence of the Realm Consolidation Act on 27 November 1914. Although it was longer, the broad content was the same. DORA contained some interesting and to us slightly odd legislation, but some of it remained in place long after the end of the war and as times changed with rapidly changing technology, by the time of the Second World War a similar piece of legislation was introduced. Some of the contents of DORA which were introduced were such things as no lighting of bonfires, letting off fireworks or flying kites. These were all seen as possible means of attracting zeppelins – not a problem that was going to persist into the Second World War, when the problem then would be enemy aircraft. The rest of the legislation was designed with two primary things in mind. One was to control the means of production and the other was to maintain the nation by denying information to the enemy. These two aims were backed up with the right of government to prosecute individuals with either summary jurisdiction for minor transgressions or, in more serious cases, courts martial. These court systems were there to cover transgressions of the legislation which fundamentally changed the social attitudes of the twentieth century. This is an important point.

Legislation by government can and does change social attitudes, since these are laws which make fundamental differences to the way in which we think

and act. This is the way in which legislation has developed during the twentieth century: as paternalistic, but sometimes misguided. One piece of legislation which we still have is for the protection of products from being counterfeit
and more recently wholesale copying of an intellectual product, such as music
or printed works.

Paternalistic help for commerce

As the Industrial Revolution became a massive producer of wealth, so the owners of recognised brands wanted, much as they do now, to protect their image
from counterfeit products of lower quality. One way of doing this is to have a
symbol, or name, which only you used, but what would stop another individual
copying the symbol? Well, nothing until the trademark was introduced as an en-
forceable item by a government which was increasingly aware that commerce
not only was important to the nation, but carried considerable weight when it
came to vexed questions. So the trademark was born in 1876. Trademark number one was not for a long-forgotten mechanism or heavy industrial company,
it was for a beer. Although used since the 1600s, trademark number one was
the red triangle of Bass Pale Ale. Interestingly this has been immortalised in the
last major work by the French artist Edouard Manet. Painted in 1882, a year
before his death, *Le Bar aux Folies-Bergeres* features exactly what it says, the
bar, tended by a rather bored-looking barmaid. On the bar can be seen a bottle
of beer with the clear red triangle of Bass on the label.

Registering a trademark in the UK is a straightforward process so long as
it fits in with certain rules. The proposed trademark must be an invented word
and must not indicate the character or the quality of goods to which it refers.
Some such nonsense words have become synonymous with the product, like
Kodak, reputedly chosen because it was a nonsense word in every language that
could be checked at the time. Another interesting example of this is the tabletop
football game known as Subbuteo. When Peter Adolph went to patent the game
he wanted it to be called 'Hobby', but this was not acceptable under the rules,
so being interested in birds he called it Subbuteo instead, which was acceptable.
Falco subbuteo is the scientific name for the bird of prey with the common name
of Hobby.

DORA introduced a series of laws which changed the way we think. No
one was allowed to talk about military matters, trespass on railway lines, feed
wild animals. The government could take over any property or factory that it

wanted for the furtherance of the war. There was also the ability to imprison without trial and censor both the spoken and printed word. Some of the rules were quite obviously of limited, or no, value, such as not being able to buy binoculars. Probably the most socially changing of these rules covered two things. The first was a change in the licensing laws for public houses. Until DORA it was possible for a pub to be open from 5.30 in the morning until half past midnight. With DORA beer was of a reduced strength and opening hours were changed from midday to 2.30 p.m. and 6.30 to 9.30 p.m. This was a big change and remained more or less so for the next 50 years. The reason for this change was declared primarily to be so that factory workers, especially munitions workers, were able to work longer hours in safety. The second change which wartime legislation brought about was in May 1916, and received the support of Winston Churchill, probably better known as the resolute leader of the resolute UK in the Second World War, also a veteran of the Boer War in South Africa as a press correspondent: namely, British Summer Time. Some of these legislations have lasted a long time and although many were dropped soon after the end of the First World War, they were modified and reintroduced during the Second World War.

During the twentieth century it became apparent that the relationship between law makers in the form of government, law enforcers and society as a whole had changed, unfortunately. When the general population was threatened by aerial attacks during the two world wars, legislation became protective, quite rightly so, being paternalistic in its intents, even when it was, with hindsight, misguided. What happened after 1950 was that paternalism increased and changed into a desire for social control by government, implementation of all this coming down to the courts.

In 1861 Parliament passed the Locomotion Act, which limited vehicles to a speed of 10 mph (about 16 km/h), which was then reduced to 4 mph in rural areas and 2 mph in towns in 1865. This was on the basis of danger to pedestrians and frightening horses. By 1896 this speed limit was increased to 14 mph and by 1930 most roads outside urban areas had no speed limit. What had been put into the hands of the masses was easy access to a lethal weapon – the car. While this was seen as necessarily controlled, it was death and carnage which introduced a speed limit in 1965 on the fastest of UK roads, the motorways, set at 70 mph, and yet there are no modern cars which cannot comfortably exceed this and many which can go twice as fast and at least one which can exceed the speed limit by a factor of three.

Following on from this, remembering that the tone of legislation was becoming, in a general sense, more controlling, there was the introduction of car seatbelts. This is undoubtedly a good thing for car drivers and their passengers. Seatbelts were in use for at least a decade before the paternalistic legislation in 1982 made front seatbelt wearing compulsory. This came into force on 31 January 1983, coinciding with the introduction of breathalysers for the measurement of alcohol. By 1991 the legislation had been extended in the UK so that rear seat passengers were obliged to wear seatbelts. While this was seen as a good thing, it is not universally so. With compulsory seatbelt wearing two things happened: the first was a reduction in death and injury to car drivers and passengers; the second was an increase in death and injury to non-car users, pedestrians and cyclists. Overall, the number of lives saved among car users was greater than the increase in deaths of non-car users, so the vulnerable lost out to the protected. The same strange attitude prevailed with the introduction of compulsory cycling helmets, which in many instances came with an increase in death and injury and a reduction in the number of cyclists, and where those who had been cyclists and now were not did not replace this exercise with anything else. The reduction in cyclists is supposedly because the helmet laws made it seem that governments were saying cycling is dangerous, without considering that it is extraordinarily rare for a cyclist to sustain head injuries just from falling off a bicycle, but relatively common when hit by a vehicle. So, again, the vulnerable are penalised for the sake of the protected. This is the problem with paternalistic legislation – it can quite easily have undesired affects.

During the twentieth century a change took place which has had repercussions down the years and will probably reform the way in which society views the law, namely implementation of science in legal cases. In many ways this was inevitable and it did, indeed, start much earlier than the twentieth century with attempts to identify individuals objectively; although a subjective assessment of whether you know someone is generally far better, the change came about when powerful scientific tools were discovered. These were primarily chemical analysis, fingerprinting and DNA profiling in all of its forms. What these latter two caused was a rethink of the interaction between individuals and the state, worldwide.

The state and judiciary now have to accept not only that there is science in their courts, but that it is driving the law, rather than merely adding weight to it. This started with the introduction of fingerprinting individuals, but had, at the end of the twentieth century, changed into something quite different. That is, we now have in many countries a legal obligation for any individual who has been stopped for any arrestable offence to give a DNA sample for analysis. The implications are profound and not widely understood. The difference is that this is no longer paternalistic legislation, but legislation designed to control the population. Sadly, many people think that this could backfire because we assume a benign regime, but should that change there will be information in the hands of government on every individual, of all sorts, which could be used destructively. Much of this will be available via the forensic science service of whichever country is involved.

In the UK, the United Kingdom Criminal Intelligence Database was set up in 1995. In 2001 the Criminal Justice and Police Act legislated that a DNA sample from anyone charged with an offence could be retained, even if they were acquitted. This was followed by creeping legislation so that the Criminal Justice Act 2003 allowed for a DNA sample to be taken on arrest, rather than on being charged. This came into force in April 2004. It also put a storage life on DNA profiles of 100 years, which is strange and illogical since, unless the intention is to change the legislation so that all newborns are DNA profiled, all arrested individuals will be dead before their profiles are disposed of. This begs the question: why keep them for so long? Well, it is probably because families can be associated together this way – all right if the regime is benign, but not if it is not. Currently the UK DNA database is the largest in the world, in part because the 2006 Police and Justice Act stated that DNA can be kept on any individual who is arrested even if they are not charged. In 2007 this was challenged in the European Court of Human Rights and was declared to be illegal, as was the holding of DNA data from those who were charged and then acquitted. This was publicly argued against by politicians who claimed that (1) most offences are caused by re-offenders (remember that they were not charged or acquitted) and (2) the innocent have nothing to fear (if they are innocent there is no reason to hold the DNA in the first place) Your genetic code is yours, it does not belong to anybody else – least of all the state. In 2006 the Identity Cards Act was also enacted, the belief being that everyone in the UK should carry a card with sufficient biometric data on it so that they can be unequivocally identified. That in itself would be difficult, but to expect individuals to pay for it would be stretching political reality rather a long way. There have been identity cards before, most notably during the First World War and then with the National Registration Act of the Second World War, which ran on for some years after the end of the war until it was finally abandoned in 1952 after criticism in the courts and a deep feeling of resentment by the populace.

This obsession by government to be able not only to identify each individual, but to have a handle on them, stems, in part, from the very earliest techniques of stating individuality – handwriting analysis and Bertillonage. Although fingerprints had been used for a very long time as statements of authenticity, for instance thumbprints were used in ancient China to verify banknotes, strictly speaking promissory notes, this was done with no formal quantification, so it was very difficult, if not impossible, to match two fingerprints to each other. Interestingly, although fingerprints were observed as individual specific, it was a much more cumbersome system which first became used as an objective measure of an individual, which eventually failed through questions of unreliability. This was a system of measurement called Bertillonage. It was introduced in 1882 by Alphonse Bertillon (1853–1914) when he was Chief of the Identification Bureau in Paris. Although it was seen as a good system, it was dogged by having to be carried out by highly trained personnel, which meant that measurements had to be made by the same individual if they were to be comparable. This is reflected in the difference between precision and accuracy, since individuals carrying out the measurements may well have had high precision but low accuracy. This is quite acceptable if it is only one person making measurements of different individuals. In general terms, however, Bertillonage was almost impossible to quantify simply because measuring biological systems is fraught with factors which are impossible to control; if you measure your height first thing in the morning you will be taller than late in the day, for example. Even though Bertillon was from a distinguished family of statisticians, the probability of two individuals sharing the same measurements was unknown and detailed techniques of statistical analysis of this type of data were simply not available at the time. The same is also true of attempts to analyse handwriting. As a technique this was discredited by the infamous Dreyfus case in France where Dreyfus, later exonerated, was accused of treason and found guilty on the basis of handwriting analysis. This disaster of justice was a product of hubris associated with a powerful individual being not just associated with the nascent science of forensic science but seen as an absolute arbiter of interpretation of scientific, and pseudo-scientific, data. See box below.

R. v. SIlverlock [1894] 2 QB 766

This is an interesting case to look at as it demonstrates the plausibility of the courts when dealing with science which may have a dubious pedigree. This case required the analysis of a handwriting sample. The question asked by the court was not 'can handwriting be identified by comparison?', which is the right question, but 'can the person giving the evidence be regarded as expert from their professional activities, or do they have to be a professional expert?', which is a complete red herring. In this case the handwriting was identified by a solicitor, having studied old handwritten documents in his spare time. Although the court was intent on deciding whether an expert was expert, it neglected to ask the big question, which was whether information given by an expert was based upon a reliable and sound foundation – was it going to mislead or help the court?

What happened in the Dreyfus case was interesting because it demonstrates the French imperialist attitude to science at the time – it had to agree with the major players in the field. There was very little peer review, just adherence to an accepted view. So, in the Dreyfus case there was a convoluted court case based on what Alphonse Bertillon said was correct – it was not.

Bertillon was a keen advocate of handwriting analysis and gave an opinion on the origin of a handwritten document. He opined that it originated from Alfred Dreyfus, then a captain in the French Army. This was in 1894 and the tested document was a letter which directly implicated the writer in an act of betrayal and resulted in Dreyfus being incarcerated for several years on the testimony of Bertillon. Perhaps even worse, when it became apparent that an error had been made, a cover-up was attempted which resulted in another officer being imprisoned on a trumped-up charge. The story takes an even more bizarre twist with the famous author Emile Zola being sentenced to a year in prison for his now famous open letter to the President of the Republic which began *J'accuse* (I accuse). Zola was lucky in that he managed to avoid incarceration by fleeing to England. With the exoneration of Dreyfus his fortunes changed and he was reinstated in his former rank in the army. His career progressed and although the First World War was not a good time for anyone, Dreyfus was promoted to lieutenant colonel.

This is the problem with many forensic techniques: they are open to rather too much subjective interpretation. Try comparing your own signature written with a soft pencil on a pad of paper and one written with a fine-point fountain pen on a single sheet of paper balanced on your knee. So where does this leave us with the history of the law? Well, it is relevant because the incorporation of these systems into law has been a mistake, but has been corrected through the passage of time.

An interesting thing about all of this sort of legislation which is trying to identify individuals exactly is that, although most would agree that there have been some spectacular results from the DNA database, with crimes being solved which would otherwise not have been, the one thing not addressed is simply this: with all this technology and legislation the crimes are still being committed in the first place. If that question was addressed it would not be necessary to have this complicated and draconian legislation in the first place, which would save a great deal of money and resentment.

2

The Legal System and How It Works

2.1 A brief look at the court structure

The legal system in the UK can be broken down into two broad categories, namely criminal cases and civil cases. Before going on to specifics of civil and criminal cases we shall look at the legal system in general. All criminal cases start off in the Magistrates' Court where preliminary hearings are conducted to determine whether the case should go to a higher court. At this stage it is unusual for any judgment to be made in serious cases, the sentencing ability of magistrates being severely limited. What does happen is that if a case is deemed too serious for the magistrates to pronounce upon themselves, it will be referred to the next stage of the court system – for criminal trials this is the Crown Court.

In civil cases it is most unusual to use the Magistrates' Court. The procedure here is to go straight to the County Court. In criminal cases in the Crown Court, where a jury is involved, any result which is questioned by the defendant can be sent to a court of appeal. This referral depends upon the nature of the complaint, so it could go from the Crown Court to the Queen's Bench Division and then on to the High Court. If it is a criminal case it would go to the Criminal Division of the Court of Appeal. After that, it becomes necessary to go to the ultimate arbiter in law, the House of Lords (see Figure 2.1).

Forensic Science in Court: The Role of the Expert Witness   Wilson Wall
© 2009 W. J. Wall

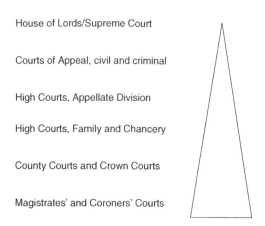

House of Lords/Supreme Court

Courts of Appeal, civil and criminal

High Courts, Appellate Division

High Courts, Family and Chancery

County Courts and Crown Courts

Magistrates' and Coroners' Courts

Figure 2.1   Court hierarchy, broadly reflected in both decision making and numbers of sitting courts, from approximately 600 Magistrates' Courts in England and Wales, through 230 County Courts to a single House of Lords.

Whatever the opinion is, the House of Lords holds justice as sacrosanct. If it has got this far, there is no further to go. When the House of Lords adjudicates for one side or another then we have to accept this as final, but, and it is a big but, only as long as there is no further or new evidence available. Should new evidence appear then it will be taken into account, even to reopening a case.

One of the many interesting aspects of the way in which the court system works is that although legislation is the exclusive providence of Parliament, courts, in the form of the judiciary, do make laws. This is not an explicit part of a judge's remit, in fact it has been explicitly stated in the distant past that judges do not make laws (this was stated in a judgment in 1892). More recently, the pendulum of opinion has moved the other way and as Lord Scarman said in a judgment in 1980, the judges have in some aspects of their work discretionary power to do justice so wide that they may be regarded as law makers. This, along with comments from other judges, was quite an astute acknowledgement of a *de facto* truth. Some rules are so general, or indeed so woolly, in their wording that a broad interpretation can be made which can result in a simple, or not so simple, common-sense interpretation of the law by the courts. It is partly for this reason that cases can so often go to a higher court for appeal. Sometimes it is necessary for a case to go to appeal simply because the wording of the original legislation is such that clarification needs to be sought just to make the law workable.

Lord Scarman

Lord Scarman (1911–2004) was an example of the traditional nature of the Law Lords, though there are of course exceptions to this pattern. Leslie George Scarman was educated first at Radley College in Oxfordshire and then at Brasenose College, Oxford where he graduated with a First in Classics. Following on from this he was called to the Bar in London, but before developing his career in law the Second World War intervened and he became a staff officer in the RAF. This led him to be present at the formal surrender of Germany at the cessation of hostilities. Returning to a career in law, Scarman became Head of the Law Commission from 1965 to 1973 and from 1977 to 1986 when he retired a Law Lord at the age of 75. During his period as a Law Lord he was not shy of controversy, upholding the conviction for blasphemy by *Gay News* in 1979 and stopping the Greater London Council programme for passenger charging 'Fares Fair' in 1981. His liberal side was also apparent in his work on behalf of the 'Birmingham Six' (see the box on this in Chapter 7).

There is one court which stands out as different to those courts already mentioned. This is the European Court of Human Rights and although a forensic scientist may be a very rare sight there, the deliberations of the court can be of very great significance to them. The European Court of Human Rights is based in Strasbourg along with the European Commission of Human Rights. The court was a direct spin-off from the European Convention of Human Rights which started life in 1950, specifically to safeguard the population from the vagaries of transgressions of human rights, most notably by governments. The court, which was finally established as a physical entity in 1959, is made up of a number of judges equal to the number of members of the Council of Europe, currently 41, which can make for a long and drawn-out legal process, but one which is invaluable. The judges generally sit for a period of six years, having been elected by the Parliamentary Assembly of the Council of Europe. Interestingly, although they come from all the signatory countries, the judges do not represent their country. The reason why a forensic scientist is unlikely to appear at the European Court of Human Rights is that it mainly undertakes an analysis of a situation in light of the European Convention of Human Rights given the evidence already supplied. So the court cannot make laws, or directly change the laws of a sovereign nation such as the UK, but it can declare a law as incompliant, effectively invalid since signatories are obliged to take notice of the decisions of the court.

European Court of Human Rights: not quite a constitution

In Chapter 1 we looked at how the laws which govern us in the UK and Commonwealth have grown in an organic way, addressing ideas and problems as they arise. This is unlike countries like the USA which effectively jumped in with both feet and produced a written constitution from scratch. This has not always been a success, partly because of problems of inflexibility.

With the institution of the European Community as a legal entity it was thought useful to have a unified Human Rights Act. Although it might appear to be a written constitution for Europe, it is simply codifying what most European nations already have in their national laws.

So instead of such bizarre ideas as a right to bear arms, which is not a right since rights are intrinsic to the individual, it is an allowance of the state given to the individual, thus we have a more measured collection of rights. These include:

- Right to life and not to be subjected to the death penalty.

- Freedom from torture.

- Freedom from slavery.

- Freedom of thought, religion and expression.

- Freedom of association.

- Liberty and security.

- Fair and public trial.

- No punishment without law, or retrospective prosecution.

This list is not exhaustive and has been tested in many national courts. Interestingly, it is unusual for cases to come before the Court of Human Rights because most cases are dealt with by national courts, which are obliged to follow the Act.

It is also worth noting that Magna Carta wandered into very specific areas, such as the measurement of cloth. This is why most of it was eroded over the centuries. It was simply outgrown because it did not deal with rights, but the situation in which the barons found themselves at the time. So although we do not have a written constitution we have a system which protects the individual as well as possible. It was in answer to the totalitarian regimes of the middle of the twentieth century in Europe that the concept of a Human Rights Act first appeared. It received Royal Ascent on 9 November 1998 and was put fully into force on 2 October 2000.

A very important part of the court system is the jury. We all have a fairly clear idea of the nature of a jury and its make-up, but like many parts of the law the independence of the jury was not automatically granted at its inception. Indeed, it would seem that as late as 1670 judges could be rather more than mere directors of the attention of the jury to the relevant facts. The change in the independence of the jury from the judge broadly came with the case of *R. v. Penn and Mead* (1670). This was unusual for many reasons. Briefly, it hinged around William Penn and William Mead. These two individuals were Quakers and inclined to ruffle establishment feathers. In the case of Penn this usually took the form of pamphlets, one of which, titled *Sandy Foundation Shaken*, published in 1669, resulted in his being thrown into the Tower of London. William Penn (1644–1718) was the son of Admiral Sir William Penn (1621–1670) and in 1681 gained title to a grant of territory in North America which was called 'Pensilvania' in honour of the admiral, later re-spelt to its modern form, and it was here that he established the city of Philadelphia. Before that, however, along with Mead he was put on trial for unlawful assembly (preaching) in Gracechurch Street, London. It was at this trial that the jury demonstrated its independence from the judge. The members of the jury were told that they would not be discharged until they had produced a verdict that was acceptable to the court. Put another way, a verdict of guilty, which would have been acceptable to the judge. The jury was locked up without food or drink for its troubles. One juror, the leader of the jury, Edward Bushell, brought the case to court. The action of the jury and the establishment of the independence of the jury was vindicated when the Lord Chief Justice Sir John Vaughan said they 'may try to open the eyes of the Jurors, but not to lead them by the nose'. This was in reference to the judges.

2.2 The adversarial system

Generally in both civil and criminal cases the method used in court is adversarial, two sides jousting with each other to persuade the court that they are right and the other side wrong. The arguments are generally made by barristers, the advocates for both sides, but it is not necessary to employ a barrister. Self-advocacy is perfectly legitimate, although it does tend to be frowned upon. I have appeared as an expert in such a case where the accused (it was a very serious criminal prosecution) was so exasperated by his barrister that he sacked him and represented himself. He was an articulate self-advocate and did in fact win, being found innocent of the charge, but this is an unusual situation, because most individuals do not have the same ability to deal with issues and witnesses as a barrister does. This brings up a point about working in court as the forensic scientist or expert witness: never take on a barrister in court. Barristers make their living using words, you make a living in analysis; however much you are provoked, stay calm and do not bandy words with the highly intelligent (they are), highly educated (they are) and highly literate (they are) barristers because you as an expert will lose.

In criminal cases the normal process is for the prosecution to be carried out on behalf of the Crown, although private prosecutions are not unknown. Papers will normally arrive with the starting statement of *R. v. XXXX*, where R. is short for Regina in the case of a queen, and Rex for a king, a lucky coincidence in that both words start with R.

There is a sort of hierarchy associated with the court system, starting with the Magistrates' Courts. There are approximately 600 Magistrates' Courts in England and Wales where approximately 28,000 magistrates deal with about 1 million cases a year. From there they may go to the Crown or County Courts. The County Courts are that by name alone, as the courts themselves are positioned in towns and cities as demand requires; there are approximately 230 County Courts in England and Wales. The Crown Court is the place where serious criminal cases are heard and consequently where the highest profile forensic evidence appears, so it is also the most common court destination for a forensic scientist giving evidence. When talking of the Crown Court it is generally referred to in the singular, because in administrative terms there is only one Crown Court, yet it sits in nearly 100 different places in England and Wales. As there are no district boundaries associated with the Crown Court, the cases which it deals with arise from the nearest Magistrates' Courts in the area. After these Crown and County Courts there are the High Courts, the Court of Appeal and finally, as the last resort, the House of Lords, until the change to a Supreme Court which should take place in October 2009. At each step there are fewer and fewer cases being looked at so that by the time we arrive at the House of Lords there are approximately 60 cases a year being reviewed.

2.3 Criminal cases

Every criminal case starts in the Magistrates' Court and up to 95% of them end there. These are summary trials, which generally involve what are regarded as minor infringements of the law, but it should be remembered that assault with a deadly weapon is very serious, even though when it is a car it is not necessarily thought so. Because the sentencing of a Magistrates' Court is limited, anything which could result in a longer than allowed custodial sentence requires that the cases goes to the next court, in the case of criminal cases the Crown Court. A summary trial is heard without a jury. It is the magistrates who decide whether they can pass judgment on a case, so consequently the judgement can be seen as arbitrary. At the Magistrates' Court it may well be required that psychological reports are prepared before a final decision is made. Within the Magistrates' Court it should be remembered that the magistrates are not necessarily qualified in law, but they will be assisted by a clerk who can, and will, give advice on matters of law. The magistrates who hear the case will be in the area in which the offence was committed. It is not necessary to have a solicitor in the Magistrates' Court, especially in minor offences when the accused simply pleads guilty. In more serious cases the procedure involving a solicitor follows a well documented flow. It starts with the prosecution outlining the case, the law and the facts to be proven. Witnesses are called in sequence and give their examination-in-chief after which they are cross-examined and then may be re-examined. Expert witnesses tend to be called last, which can result in a lot of hanging around. The defence lawyer may say to the court that there is no case to answer. If this is accepted the case ends, if not then the defence case proceeds. Defence counsel has to make a decision as to whether to make an opening or a closing speech. After the defence witnesses have given their evidence the bench announces a decision (not the wooden structure, you understand, but the magistrates). If it is decided that the accused is guilty and the sentence is within the remit of the court, it will be passed. If an appeal is lodged on the basis of law or fact it can be heard in the Crown Court; if it is on law only it will generally go to the Divisional Court of the High Court. In the Crown Court there will be no jury and the whole proceedings will start from scratch all over again. If the expert evidence is given at the Magistrates' Court and the case proceeds to the Crown Court it is important to remember that there is no official record of what is said in the Magistrates' Court – though it is highly likely that someone will have made informal notes. These may be used as a basis of your cross-examination in the Crown Court, so be very precise about what you said as it is always possible that the notes were not entirely correct, and when transcribed and given to the barrister gradually drift from what was actually said and what was meant by you.

Once the magistrates have decided that the charge is beyond their sentencing ability, the case will go to the Crown Court, at which the trial is referred to as an indictment. The way in which a Crown Court trial by jury is conducted is very similar to the way a Magistrates' Court proceedings is carried out, but it is done in a rather more formal way. It starts when the defendant is arraigned, with the charges being read out in open court by the clerk of the court. If the defendant pleads guilty at this point the trial is effectively finished and it only remains for the judge to pass sentence. If the defendant pleads not guilty, the case starts in earnest with the jury being empanelled. Although the jury will have been sworn in, either side of the case may ask for an application to be made on a preliminary point of law. This will be heard in the absence of the jury, as will any request for evidence to be excluded.

Just as in the Magistrates' Court, the case opens with the prosecution stating the case which has to be proved. This involves outlining the elements of the law which have been infringed. It also includes details of the evidence upon which the Crown (the normal prosecutor in criminal cases in the form of the Crown Prosecution Service (CPS)) will rely upon for their case. As well as this, there is the most important point that the jury should not try and decide matters of law; these are matters for the judge. The jury decides upon matters of fact. Although it may seem that the giving of evidence is haphazard, this should not be the case. Witnesses are called in such a way that there is a logical flow, such that the entire story is unfolded in the way in which it happened. It starts with the prosecution calling witnesses in a uniform flow. Each witness is cross-examined by the opposing counsel, the defence in the first instance and the prosecution when the defence starts to call their witnesses.

The general structure of the proceedings in a criminal trial is quite formal and can be broadly summarised thus:

1. Opening speech by the prosecution.

2. Prosecution call their evidence dealing with witnesses:

   (a) Examination-in-chief (prosecution)

   (b) Cross-examination (defence)

   (c) Re-examination (prosecution).

At this point the defence may claim 'no case to answer'. If the court agrees, the defendant goes free, if not, the case proceeds.

1. Defence opening speech.

2. Defence call their evidence dealing with witnesses:

   (a) Examination-in-chief (defence)

   (b) Cross-examination (prosecution)

   (c) Re-examination (defence).

3. Defence closing speech.

4. Optional prosecution closing speech.

Expert witnesses may sit in court and listen to all the evidence.

2.4 The expert

In the case of an agreement regarding an expert report in criminal cases this will usually originate from the Forensic Science Service and, if the results are not disputed, for example if the defendant pleads guilty when faced with the report, it is quite possible that the expert will not be required to attend court, both parties agreeing the results of the expert investigation. The evidence in this case is simply read to the court, but is as important as if the expert was in court in person. On the other hand, if there is continual denial on the part of the defendant, or counsel has questions about the report, an independent report may be commissioned. As an expert you should take heed of what your counsel suggests, but do not be swayed by suggestions made by counsel – it is your report and yours alone.

It is quite normal for an expert to sit in upon a case, though there may be objections from one side or another. Do not be irritated by this, it is all part of the hurly-burly of how a court works; it is no reflection on either you or your subject, whatever it might be.

Just as in a Magistrates' Court, when the counsel for the prosecution has finished the defence may suggest to the judge that the prosecution have not proved all the elements of the offence, so there is no charge to answer. This has to be done in the absence of the jury for the obvious reason that such suggestions made in the presence of the jury could prejudice the outcome of the trial. Remember that at all times the court wants to know the truth, not a prejudiced version of events. If a judge decides that there is no case to answer, the judge will direct the jury to find the accused 'not guilty'. This is not a silly point, because it is the jury which decides the outcome of any trial of this sort, not the judge; this is the whole point of having a jury. If the case continues, the way in which it is conducted depends upon the defence calling witnesses.

2.5 Witnesses

When calling witnesses besides the defendant, defence counsel may make an opening speech to the jury; if the defendant is representing themselves, which is quite in order if a little unusual, the defendant will give evidence first. No matter what, the giver of evidence will be cross-examined. This is all part and parcel of an adversarial system trying to determine the truth of an allegation which may result in the loss of liberty of an individual.

2.6 Judgments

As the Crown Court deals with the most severe cases it has always been in-cumbent upon it to be as sure as possible when handing down judgments. This cannot have been more difficult than when obliged to declare the use of the death penalty. This was abolished in the UK in 1965 upon which it became normal for the trial judge and the Lord Chief Justice to recommend how long the individual should serve in custody – but it is the Home Secretary who actually fixes the term. An example of this is the case where there were a series of murders and rapes in a small village in Leicestershire. The man found guilty was Colin Pitchfork, who received 10 years for each rape, to run concurrently, much to the horror of the families, but the Lord Chief Justice then set the tariff to 30 years. In the middle of 2004 the Law Commission described the law on murder as a 'mess' and suggested that the law should be reformed with a view to different levels of murder, such as mercy killing and self-defence.

Just as in the case of the Magistrates' Court, the case for the prosecution is laid out first, at the beginning of the trial. If the defendant is acting as their own counsel and is going to give evidence on their own behalf, this evidence is heard first, after the prosecution case has been laid out, after which the defendant is cross-examined like any other witness. If the defendant is being represented and counsel chooses to call the defendant, this is normally done last. After the concluding speeches, first by the Crown (prosecution) and then the defence, the judge gives a summing up for the benefit of the jury. The purpose of this is to direct the jury on points of law, and to remind the jury of significant aspects of the evidence. This is not so strange as it might sound because a serious case may well take place over several days and it is the judge who takes note of the proceedings in court for precisely this reason. The court reporter will produce a verbatim record of what was said and done, but this is usually too long and verbose to be of use to the members of the jury, even if it was available for them to see it in time for them to deliberate on the case. Once the jury has retired (not in the bus pass sense) to consider its verdict, there is a set sequence which can be adhered to, at the discretion of the judge. When initially told to retire and consider the verdict, the outcome has to be unanimous. After two hours the judge can, at any time, direct the jury to accept a majority verdict. This process does depend upon the severity of the charge, but will always require that at least 10 of the 12 jurors agree on the verdict. Once the verdict is agreed upon by the jury, the jury returns to the body of the court and the foreman of the jury declares the collective decision. If this is innocent then the defendant is acquitted; if it is guilty the judge will determine and pass sentence, usually carried out at a later date to give time for the judge to assess any psychiatric reports and the severity of the charge, and therefore the severity of the sentence. It is always possible to ask for leave to appeal; in the most serious of cases this is quite common.

2.7 Justification of the expert

Now, having looked at the structure of the legal system the immediate question must be 'what is the legal justification for expert witnesses?' Well, it starts from the assumption, which is in itself self-evident, that we cannot all be expert in all things. We might like to think we are, in the same way as we think that our parents know everything, but in a court of law our fallibility will be revealed. Do not step out of your discipline. Do not be tempted to make a declaration that can be shown to be beyond your remit; the cross-examining counsel might try to tempt you to do this, but there is absolutely nothing wrong in saying that it is beyond your expertise.

Frye v. United States

In 1923 the Supreme Court ruled that unsubstantiated scientific evidence was legally inadmissible. This has led to what is now described as the Frye test, basically whether the forensic evidence stands up as scientifically valid in its own right. This was based on a challenge to the scientific validity of the polygraph, or lie detector. This is a poor relation to Bertillonage and should have been abandoned a long time ago as little more than pseudo-science.

The ruling was basically that scientific evidence could only be admitted to court if it was 'sufficiently established to have gained general acceptance in the particular field in which it belongs'. The case was based around the measurement of blood pressure as a lie detector and since this was not widely accepted by scientists it was regarded as inadmissible. This was generally refined in the case of *Daubert* v. *Merrell Dow Pharmaceuticals*.

Daubert v. Merrell Dow Pharmaceuticals

This case set the legal precedent in the US Supreme Court, in 1993, with regard to the admissibility of the testimony of an expert witness. Fundamentally the ruling was that expert witnesses must be evaluated as to whether their testimony is both reliable and relevant. This tightened up the old idea of the Frye test by suggesting that the test must be falsifiable, subjected to peer review and publication, with a known error rate and also, as with Frye, generally recognised as sound by the scientific community. This last point does tend to assume something more than it says because the question always remains 'what is the scientific community?'

So the question remains 'who constitutes an expert witness?' Well you do, in whatever field you are expert in (see the box above). You do not need to be formally qualified because, after all, it is unlikely that any lawyer would be able to find a formally qualified individual who can give evidence on a subject such as the construction of a flat-pack piece of furniture into its rightful shape. But many individuals are well versed in this process and some may be so well acquainted with the process that they can realistically be called 'expert'. It is sometimes said that experts are those that have qualifications and experience which enable them to give opinions on the facts in a specific case. But qualifications may not be appropriate, or, as cited previously, relevant or possible to obtain. This does not, however, proscribe an individual from being an expert. This was clarified many years ago, starting at the end of the eighteenth century with *Folkes* v. *Chadd* in which Lord Mansfield said that it was not necessary that the expert gained his understanding in any particular way, the implication here being formal education. This flexibility of attitude is reinforced by a witness, in this case a lawyer, being allowed to comment upon handwriting as he had made a study of the subject, over many years, as a hobby. It should be realised, however, that as time has moved on, the ability to gain a formal qualification in all manner of subjects has become commonplace. Consequently it has become evermore difficult to persuade a court that you are an expert. It is now both a qualification and working practice which define an expert. Some areas of work do not lend themselves to formal qualifications, such as the manufacture of soap, but in the twenty-first century these are few and far between and becoming ever rarer. The arcane word which is used to define an expert is *peritus*, a Latin word that can be roughly translated as 'skilled or expert'. It is for historical reasons that so much Latin is used, probably no longer necessary for lawyers thinking that complicated use of words validates their position, much as medical doctors do now. Anyway, prove *peritus* (i.e. expert) and you will be taken as an expert. Attitudes towards the expert have changed considerably (see box below).

> **Abinger v. Ashton [1874] 22 WR 582**
>
> This is a case which demonstrates the early disbelief in the integrity of expert evidence. It is summed up with a quote from the judge in the case, Sir George Jessel: 'In matters of opinion I very much distrust expert evidence, for several reasons.' He then goes into several of his reasons, mostly regarding payment of fees. One can only assume he had no notion of scientific integrity but a clear one of the mercenary.

At this juncture there is a significant point which has to be made: the difference between a witness of fact and a witness of opinion. A witness of fact is a person who gives evidence regarding something they themselves have either seen or heard. A witness of opinion gives evidence that has not been directly observed, the evidence of the expert.

Most cases involving a criminal charge are brought by the state against an individual, but not always. I was myself involved in the private prosecution of the individuals associated with the death of Steven Lawrence. In all cases which involve the Crown, it is the decision of the CPS as to what the charge is, not the police. It is also the CPS which decides whether there is a charge to answer.

2.8 Civil cases

Civil disputes are cases in which one party seeks redress from another, where no criminal proceedings are carried out.

It was at a civil case involving a fire on board a ship, the *Ikarian Reefer* (see box below), that Mr Justice Cresswell outlined his ideas on the duties and responsibilities of an expert in a civil case. These included:

- Expert evidence should be seen to be independent, regardless of the form of the litigation.

- The expert must be unbiased and assist the court in coming to a conclusion.

- The expert must state any assumptions or facts upon which the expert's conclusions are based.

- The expert should make it clear when a question is beyond their expertise.

- The expert must say whether there was sufficient data for the conclusion, or if not then make it clear that the opinion was provisional.

National Justice Compania Naviera S.A. v. Prudential Assurance Company Ltd (Ikarian Reefer)

Aboard the ship the *Ikarian Reefer* a fire broke out in the engine room causing considerable damage. The question was whether, as claimed by the owners, this was an insurable loss and therefore a claim was valid, or, as the underwriters claimed, the fire had been started deliberately, with the connivance or knowledge of the owners of the vessel, in which case no insurance claim could be made.

After reports have been exchanged, if one of the experts has a change of mind, then this should be communicated to the other side by a legal representative.

All material of fact, such as plans and other documents, must be provided to the other side at the same time as the reports are exchanged.

This last point, exchange of reports and factual data upon which is based an agreement, a disagreement or a final outcome, is of particular interest as indicated by Lord Donaldson: 'litigation is not a war or even a game. It is designed to do real justice between opposing parties and, if the court does not have all the relevant information, it cannot achieve this object.' So always be open and honest when dealing with a court and experts on the other side.

The first thing that an expert witness should do is produce a preliminary report. This does not need to be shown to the other side as only reports which are going to be used in court need to be revealed to the other side. The preliminary report should give all the strengths and weaknesses of the case, as painting a rosy picture to the plaintiff and their lawyers will only cause problems later. With the preliminary report the lawyer can advise the plaintiff as to whether it would be worth going to litigation. Should the report be unfavourable, but the lawyer or plaintiff still wants to pursue litigation, it is not necessary for the unfavourable report to be disclosed to the defendant as it will not be used in court.

There are two civil courts where civil trials are held. These are the County Courts and the High Court. Most civil cases never come to court. These are usually claims for faulty goods, personal injury, landlord/tenant and professional injury. Small claims are also dealt with by the County Courts, although if a hearing is held it is informal before a district judge. There is no legal aid for small claims and the only way recovery of costs can be made is by going to court. This is an area of particular interest to experts as defaulting payment from solicitors is not uncommon and they frequently have to be taken to the Small Claims Court. If you have insisted upon a letter of instruction with the agreed sum on it, there is no defence and the sum is usually passed automatically. If it comes into dispute it becomes a little more complicated, as will be described in more detail in Chapter 6.

Disputed claims where the sums are less than £5000 are heard in the County Court by a district judge. Sums great than that are heard by an assistant recorder, a recorder or a circuit judge.

Forms of address

Assistant recorder, recorder, or a circuit judge are addressed as Sir or Madam. A circuit judge is referred to as Your Honour.

In a civil court the way in which a trial takes place is slightly different from a criminal trial. In a civil court proceedings are most often referred to as a hearing, rather than a trial, and the process is not so much about an individual having committed some sort of offence which the state deems to be unacceptable, such as theft, assault, rape, murder, but an attempt to settle an argument. This is often not easy: a judge judges, but it is not always easy being obliged to come to a decision, just as a referee has to in a football match – civil cases are very similar.

Civil court hearings, either in the High Court or County Court, generally take the same format. It is in the civil courts that the expert witness can find themselves unseated. While in criminal cases the outcome tends to be a matter of fact, in civil cases the case will often hinge more upon persuasion than fact.

The start of a case in a civil court begins with the plaintiff, or counsel for the complainant, making an opening speech. This should give details of the facts of the claim and areas of dispute and agreement. It should be realised that as an independent expert, if you cannot see any problem with the arguments, or point, of the opposing side, you must tell counsel. Do not jeopardise your credibility by saying yes when you should have said no. This is exactly the same as in criminal prosecutions: do not write or say something you cannot justify. The plaintiff, or their counsel, will state the facts of the complaint, as seen by the plaintiff. This could be something like a broken contract, defaulted payment, bad professional advice, or a physical injury sustained in an accident. All of these turn on a single question which is simply put, but more difficult to resolve: 'how much is it worth in monetary terms?' The forensic scientist will occasionally be asked to address that particular question, but most likely will be asked to give evidence as to the apparent truth behind the claim. It is the assessment of liability which is most important for the forensic scientist or expert witness. An example of a situation where an expert, in this case not necessarily a forensic scientist, is asked to help the court in its entirety would be where a car was damaged by a falling roof tile while being serviced in a garage. Was this due to severe weather or inadequate building maintenance, implying liability? If the court decides it was neglect the expert may be asked for an opinion of what the cost of the repair might be.

During this initial submission the legal representation, whether it is a barrister, solicitor or an advocate of any sort, reference is made to any legal authorities which may be relevant to the case. To those involved in, or likely to be involved in, civil cases I would suggest that they read an extremely witty book, *Uncommon Law*, by A. P. Herbert, published by Independent Publishing Group (2001). This takes some of the wind from the sails of overly complicated legal arguments.

In civil cases the counsel for the claimant will draw attention to any correspondence, whether this is plans, photographs or just documents and letters (see also Figure 2.2). Given that in civil cases each side will have instructed their own expert, it is necessary that that expert evidence is either agreed or not. The possibility is also that a single joint witness will be appointed by the court itself. If both counsel agree that the burden depends upon the defendant, the procedure can be altered, which may result in the defendant opening the case first, rather than the claimant.

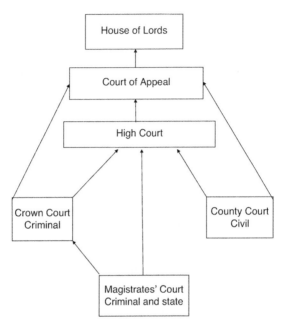

Figure 2.2 A simple representation of the flow of information, cases, through the court system. Note that civil cases do not normally start in the Magistrates' Court. Arrows reflect the appeal system.

Given a normal procedure within the court, counsel for the claimant starts proceedings. This will commence with the calling of witnesses, in a consistent order. The complainant usually goes first, but after that it should be a process of both logic and the flow of events which gave rise to the complaint. After giving evidence-in-chief, the claimant can generally stand down, unless circumstances have changed since the original statement was made.

After the claimant has given evidence it is the turn of the defendant. Should the case be found against the defendant an order to pay damages will be made. This in no way infers guilt, simply the liability of the defendant for damage incurred. Interestingly, when the defendant is insured the defence is frequently run by the defendant's insurers; the larger the claim, the more likely this is to be the case. Results in civil cases can be appealed against should it be thought necessary.

When questioned, an expert witness (you) will have to be precise, accurate and your evidence defensible – defensible because it is your evidence which may alter the course of a trial You should not, ever, say anything except that which is truthful, and if you see a wrongdoing it is your right and duty to stand up and say so, in court and to the judge, whose right it is to give you absolute protection.

Since the expert's reports will have been seen by both sides of the dispute under rules of prior disclosure, cross-examination of witnesses is quite normal and will, or should, be relevant to the case, or attempt to discredit the expert as an expert in whatever field is under discussion. After the case for the claimant has been heard, the case for the defence starts. Now, counsel for the claimant is able to re-examine the witness, be they an expert or any other sort, such as a witness of fact. Because civil actions can be quite complicated and time consuming with claims and counterclaims, there is a general time limit put upon them. This takes the form of close of pleadings, after which no more claims or counterclaims can be made. The general procedure of a civil claim takes the following route:

1. The plaintiff, or the plaintiff's advocate, gives an opening speech, setting out the facts and the consequent issues of the case. Very occasionally the defence may make an opening speech at this point.

2. Witnesses for the plaintiff are called. Each will be given examination- in-chief by the plaintiff or their advocate, followed by cross-examination by the lawyer for the defence. If anything new has appeared during the cross-examination the witness can be re-examined by the lawyer for the plaintiff. This is to help clarify the situation for the court.

3. The witnesses for the defendant are examined and cross-examined and possibly re-examined in the same way as the witnesses for the plaintiff are.

4. A closing speech is made by the defence, followed by a speech by the plaintiff's lawyer.

2.9 Magistrates' Court

Once the decision has been made to prosecute, the procedure is well defined. If the charge is not serious, such as minor shoplifting offences, parking offences and other minor or petty crimes, these will be seen in the Magistrates' Court. If the criminal case is heard completely in the Magistrates' Court it is called a summary trial. It is thought that approximately 95% of trials of a criminal type are summary. It is relatively unusual for an expert to be present in the Magistrates' Court.

Summary trials can be heard by a stipendiary magistrate, who may be a district judge, a solicitor or a barrister, as long as they have at least seven years' experience. The other alternative is three lay magistrates, with training but no formal legal qualifications. They are volunteers, sometimes referred to as justices of the peace. These are supported on points of law by a legally qualified magistrates clerk.

Forms of address

Magistrates are addressed as either Sir or Madam. It should be noted, however, that a novice expert or forensic scientist will not be penalised for using Sir or Madam in any court, even if this is not necessarily a correct form of address.

There are some rules. An expert for the prosecution is most likely called last, the defence expert usually gets to give evidence first. There is no obvious reason why the experts should not both be in court at the same time, although this does not generally happen in Magistrates' Courts. In court after the defence has presented their case they can state that there is no case to answer. It is now the chance for the prosecution to make a statement. It should be remembered that for minor cases, such as minor motoring offences, counsel will not necessarily be required, especially where the defendant pleads guilty. While a district judge may have no doubt in their mind, it is usual for a lay bench to retire to decide the verdict. If guilty the bench will pronounce the sentence, currently a maximum custodial sentence of six months and normally a maximum fine of £5000; however, in serious cases, usually of an environmental nature such as pollution of a watercourse, this can be as much as £20,000. In serious cases where it is thought by the magistrates that they do not have sufficient sentencing powers, or the defendant lodges an appeal, there are several routes that the case can take. Although it may sound straightforward that there a number of different routes, the courts tend to deal in different ways. The normal procedure at the next stage is for the case to be heard in the Crown Court.

2.10 The Crown Court

After the Magistrates' Court comes the Crown Court. The start of the trial is by arraignment, which is carried out by reading out an indictment, a simple case of reading out in court what the charges are. There is a jury present and serious crimes include murder, serious assaults, including rapes, fraud and drug offences. Presiding may be a circuit judge, a high court judge or a recorder.

In the case of the defendant pleading guilty it is the job of the judge at that point to sentence the self-confessed guilty individual. No jury is required in this situation. It is quite different where the defendant pleads not guilty. Then a jury is required which is made up of 12 individuals.

There are exceptions as to who is allowed to sit on a jury. These include members of government, ministers of certain denominations, practising barristers, solicitors, registered medical practitioners, dentists and officers and soldiers. There are also a number of people who, though not disqualified, are exempt from jury service.

The judge hearing the case has to direct the jury on points of law and also indicate how much weight various pieces of evidence should be given. It is always the jury that decides guilt or innocence. Before the trial starts properly, either the defence or prosecution counsel can ask for the judge to make a decision of law, or exclusion of some evidence, which will be done in the absence of the jury. In criminal cases it is the counsel for the prosecution which open the case for the Crown. They have to prove the evidence which the defence which will try and rebut. The judge gives the barristers the burden and standard of proof; this is what needs to be proved and the level at which it needs to be proved. The evidence should be presented in a consistent manner to tell the story of events. After giving their evidence-in-chief, either for the prosecution or the defence, the witness will be cross-examined. If any points are raised on cross-examination a re-examination can take place. This is not as unusual as it sounds and it is most likely to take place when an expert is being used in court, for the simple reason that it can be very difficult for a court, in all its forms, to follow difficult technical points. Some experts are natural communicators and can put across complicated points easily. Sadly, communication skills are not routinely taught.

The matters of law regarding the case should always be referred to the judge. Usually it is the expert that is the last witness to be called. This does sometimes make for long waits because it is not always easy to estimate how long a court case will take and it can be very frustrating to go to court for, say, two days, expecting to be called at any time, only to find that the case collapses before you can give your evidence. It is also possible that if there are no contested points in a written report, by either side, the report can be simply read out in court. This does not mean it is in any way a lesser report. Reports and writing them will be dealt with later. Having a report read out in court saves the expert time and an overall reduction in costs. If the defence wish to call an additional witness later, after the start of the trial, special leave has to be sought from the judge, if it involves undisclosed papers.

Forms of address

These depend on who is sitting and the status, but all judges in a Crown Court, whether they are assistant recorders, recorders or circuit judges, are addressed as Your Honour and on court lists have the abbreviation HHJ after their name. Exceptions to this are high court judges (sometimes referred to as red judges due to the colour of their robes). Any judges sitting at the Old Bailey have the abbreviation J after their name on court lists as do those in the Court of the Recorders of both Liverpool and Manchester. These are all addressed as Your Lordship or Ladyship, sometimes My Lord or My Lady.

2.11 The High Court

Appeals made at the High Court may sometimes be heard in the Queen's Bench Division of the High Court. These appeals are carried out by one high court judge and one lord justice of appeal.

Forms of address

Both a high court judge and a lord justice of appeal should be addressed as Your Lordship or Your Ladyship. Sometimes as My Lord or My Lady.

2.12 The Courts of Appeal

The High Court hears appeals from the Magistrates' Court or the Crown Court. This is presided over by one high court judge and one lord justice of appeal.

The Criminal Division of the Court of Appeal hears appeals from Crown Courts on matters of law, but can also take action in appeals against sentence made by either the prosecution or defence. Covering the appeals there are usually three individuals, although two can sit without the third. Of these three at least one must be a lord justice of appeal, the other two might be two further lord justices of appeal, or, alternatively, two high court judges, or one high court judge and one circuit judge.

Finally an appeal may be heard by the House of Lords, after which nothing more can be done. Appeals are heard from the Court of Appeal and exceptionally the High Court. There are usually from three to seven, but usually five, lords of appeal hearing the case.

Forms of address

Whatever combination is used, the correct form of address is either Your Lordship or Your Ladyship. Alternatively it could be shortened to My Lord or My Lady.

There are two other areas which have codes of law attached to them: one is the Coroner's Court and the other is formal tribunals.

Forms of address

All sitters in these courts are either Sir or Madam.

2.13 Small Claims Court

Any amount can be claimed in the Small Claims Court, which is part of the County Court. Cases of lower amounts, usually less than £5000, are heard in an informal hearing. In small claims there is no legal aid available. Court costs are generally awarded to the successful claimant but are limited, so expert witnesses are rarely called. With very large sums the hearings are held by an assistant recorder, recorder or circuit judge.

Forms of address

Assistant recorder, recorder and district judge are all addressed as either Sir or Madam. A circuit judge is addressed as Your Honour.

2.14 Arbitration

Arbitration is strictly speaking not a judicial procedure, as it is operating outside the courts. It reaches a conclusion that is binding on both parties. In civil cases where proceedings do not exceed a claim of £1000, a defence to the claim is filed. It is necessary to be sure that you have a good chance of a happy resolution because legal aid is not available in these cases.

Because the arbitration service carries out investigations in a very informal way, it can come to a conclusion with more speed than if proceedings were taken through the normal, more formal channels of the courts.

Arbitration makes a great deal of use of expert evidence in all manner of ways and in all areas where specialised expertise is required to inform the arbiter. It does follow that one of the very good reasons for holding the arbitration in private is that when the parties are in dispute regarding a matter, of, say, business, discussions may reveal details which may be of considerable advantage to other traders. It is even true that, unless the relevant parties wish it to be known, the very fact of there being an arbitration will remain out of the public domain.

It is often the case that the parties to the arbitration will pick their own arbiter, who can be a lawyer, or someone who might be an individual familiar with the field in which the disagreement has taken place, perhaps an engineer or veterinary surgeon. It is incumbent on the arbitration procedure to keep costs down and speed proceedings up, but unfortunately this does not always happen. Arbitration starts at the point when both parties agree it should; failing that, written notice can be given by one or the other requiring the agreement of the appointment of an arbiter. The basics of arbitration were laid down in the Arbitration Act 1996.

If you consider the nature of arbitration you may realise how difficult it can be to reach an agreement between two individuals who could not come to an agreement between themselves. The objects are, broadly, to obtain a fair and impartial resolution of the dispute. The next point is that any resolution must be in the public interest, where necessary, and the disputing parties should be able to agree on how the dispute may be resolved. Courts should not interfere except in exceptional circumstances.

Where an expert is appointed, it is important that they are fully informed of the rules and agreed procedures for that particular arbitration hearing. Arbitration procedures are in the hands of the parties involved and consequently they all tend to differ slightly. All parties involved must be able to correct any opinion. Arbitration hearings are not legal aided, so the arbiters are liable for the fees. It is therefore essential that the expert makes sure that they have a proper terms of agreement so that there is no possibility of default on payments.

It is possible for the arbiter also to be an expert in the area of the argument, and as such may be required to pass comment and be asked questions as expert, but must always be seen to be impartial and disinterested (do not confuse uninterested with disinterested – refer to a dictionary if you are unsure). It is important that an expert sitting as arbiter should not contradict an expert appointed by the arbiters, as this would undermine the ultimate decision. It is essential that both parties feel that they are appearing before a neutral individual whom they can both trust.

When an expert appears before an arbitration, absolute neutrality is essential. During this section it has been implied that arbitration takes place between individuals, but the reality is that it can be between an individual and a corporation, two corporations, or a corporation and a local or national authority.

The arbiter has what can be the onerous task of making a decision that may well leave one or other of the arbiters not completely satisfied, just prepared to compromise.

2.15 The Coroner's Court

This is included here more for interest than practicality as forensic evidence is rarely called. The office of coroner is a very ancient one and has been very significant in law enforcement. Although in England it has probably been a *de facto* position for a thousand years, it was not until 1194 that it was clearly stated that there would be three knights and a clerk to 'keep the pleas of the Crown'. This was aimed at making sure that money due to the Crown, in the first instance Richard I, did not disappear into the pockets of the local sheriff. The association with the king turned the job title into Crowner, which over time became coroner. Although the British Empire exported the position of coroner, it was in the UK itself that the coroner's position was steadily regulated until in 1926 the Coroners Amendment Act more or less defined the position as we have it now. The coroner conducts an inquest into all deaths occurring by violent or unnatural means or for some unknown or unexpected reason. The Act also stipulated that the coroner should be a legally qualified medical practitioner, a barrister or a solicitor. The coroner does not work alone as there is also a coroner's jury which may consist of between 7 and 11 members There are currently 157 Coroners' Courts in England and Wales, with 21 of these being full time. The bulk of the work involves unnatural or unexpected deaths and violent deaths. The coroner may order a post-mortem to identify the cause of death and if it is felt necessary an inquest, for example if the death occurred in the custody of either the police or prison. The number of referrals to the coroner is about 45% of annual deaths, 50% of which result in a post-mortem and of those approximately 25% result in an inquest. It is generally only those which become the topic of inquests that are of interest to the public at large and the press as they generally represent the rare and unusual.

2.16 Courts martial

It has long been the tradition that the military in all its forms has its own legal system. This has many shortcomings, if only because a system designed to be used during times of war does not sit comfortably in a peacetime regime. The use of courts martial has also been seen as both arbitrary and severe. In the twenty-first century the procedure of a court martial is much the same as for a civilian court. Historically the system started in the thirteenth century with the king issuing the Rules and Ordinances of War at the start of a campaign, of which there were many. This set of rules was the basis of the military law for military offences. The offences have not significantly changed, being based around cowardice and desertion, but what has changed is the punishment. For several centuries it broadly took the form of punitive punishment such as death, flogging and mutilation. It was only in 1689 that military courts were legally recognised; until this point members of the armed forces were regarded as personal retainers of the sovereign and therefore military justice came from the king rather than Parliament. Even after this time the procedure of a court martial was essentially hidden. Regimental Courts Martial were brief, sentences were carried out without delay and until 1805 there was no written record. Until this time it was normal for no oath to be taken by members of the court or witnesses. General Courts Martial were rather more formal and had records submitted to the sovereign or commander-in-chief, either of whom could vary the sentence as they desired. The members of the court also swore an oath.

By the twentieth century there were four different courts martial. Two of these could not try an officer, but a General Court Martial could try an officer of any rank and had the power of life and death. There was also at this time a Field General Court Martial for those on active service. Considering the extreme power of this court, it is somewhat surprising that it only needed three members, or two if that was all that were available. It was this sort of court that was used in the field throughout the years of the First World War on the western front. The Field General Courts Martial that were held during the years 1914–1918 found a total of more than 3000 servicemen on active duty guilty of a number of different crimes and passed the sentence of death. In these cases, before the sentence is carried out it should be confirmed by a superior authority – in fact,11% of these sentences were confirmed.

Since 1954 it has been possible for the accused to appeal on a point of law, but not against the sentence. The appeal is heard by the Courts Martial Appeal Court, which is made up of civilian judges from the Court of Appeal.

2.17 Contempt

An area which it is important for the forensic scientist to know about is contempt. There are two types of contempt, Common Law Contempt and the Contempt of Court Act 1981. Both of these are associated with stopping a court case from being prejudiced by what someone might hear or read about an accused if they are associated with the case, specifically a member, or potential member, of the jury. Other types of contempt take place within the court itself. There are civil contempt of court situations, but these are primarily to do with failure to comply with a court order. Although some of the aspects of contempt may not appear to be of direct importance to the forensic scientist, it is worth remembering that the court is a charged environment and outbursts can happen, sometimes even provoked. The Contempt of Court Act 1981 was introduced to limit the contempt rule and to try and bring it into line with rulings on contempt by the European Court, specifically Article 10 of the Human Rights Act, which covers freedom of expression. It should of course be remembered that there is a world of difference between freedom of expression and slander or libel, both of which are separate offences and revolve around unfounded accusations. The introduction of the Act was a direct result of the ruling in the House of Lords in the case of the *Attorney General* v. *Times Newspapers Ltd* (1974) in which it was suggested that the reporting of the case of the victims of Thalidomide by the *Sunday Times* was in contempt because discussion in the press amounted to prejudgment of the case and it would therefore undermine the authority of the court. The European Court ruled that the restrictions that had been imposed were unnecessary and would have restricted public discussion of the case. Although Thalidomide was of no value for its original intended purpose as a method of controlling morning sickness in pregnancy, the side effects being severe physical birth defects, it has found uses elsewhere. After it was withdrawn, it was by chance found to be of unique benefit in treating some of the complications of leprosy and later still it is also of value as a treatment for a very difficult cancer, multiple myeloma.

In the Contempt of Court Act 1981 there are essentially three areas where an individual can raise the ire of the court. The first of these takes place within the court itself. This area encompasses abuse of the court and those taking part in the proceedings, or, put another way, swearing or hurling insults at the judge, jury members, witnesses or other officials, also the court process. Another area in this category is abusing or interfering with the court proceedings, which could take the form of the accused attacking a member of staff, or witness, or one witness attacking another. It is up to the court to decide if any particular activity falls into this category of contempt and what sanction, if any, should be made against the individual responsible. It is also possible to lodge an appeal against a charge of contempt made for this type of transgression.

The second type of contempt, as with the third type, is essentially about published words covering the court case. This deals with any act or published writing that reduces the authority of the judge. It could be inferred that even allegations of a miscarriage of justice could be seen as contempt, but in practice this does not happen, even when on occasion this has, by its nature, implied judicial bias. On the other hand, a real or implied allegation of incorrect motives of the judge has been declared a case of contempt. Here again there is leeway in interpretation of the rules with a well reasoned argument for the allegation of improper motives being less likely to incur a charge of contempt; the more robust and self-confident the judiciary is as a whole, the less likely it is that charges of contempt will be laid.

Possibly the major area in which contempt can occur is the printed reporting of a case in progress. This is an important aspect of the law because it is specifically there to stop court proceedings being prejudiced or influenced by reporting in the media – basically anything which influences the fairness of a trial.

With Common Law Contempt of court the situation is slightly different because there does not even need to be a trial in progress at the time of the offence of contempt. A situation where this may arise is when an individual is named in the press before arrest – perhaps in the case of a blackmailer or a person holding hostages. This would be further compounded by any mention of the person's background or previous convictions. It is generally accepted that Common Law Contempt does generally require demonstration of a specific intent to commit contempt, so even here there is some flexibility in the application of the rules.

As can be imagined, the case of contempt in print both before and during a trial, but especially during, can be of considerable significance for the forensic scientist. A case should never be discussed with anyone. In fact it should be axiomatic that a forensic scientist should never pass an opinion on a court case and should never discuss such matters with even friends or family. It is a good habit to get into, because you can never be sure where idle remarks may end up. As we shall see in Chapter 7, dealing with ethics, there is a very great responsibility placed upon forensic scientists regarding their integrity.

3

Rules of Evidence as They Apply to an Expert Witness

Rules regarding evidence can be quite complicated, so the first thing we need to do is define what we mean by evidence. This usually is thought of as a means to prove or disprove some sort of disputed fact in a trial held before a court or other tribunal. The rules of evidence broadly describe what is admissible in court and what can be introduced. Rules of evidence are not rigid, as they can be modified as different cases appear in court, especially with new technology constantly appearing. This flexibility means that new techniques can be used as evidence, or the court can dispute the validity of the technique, or science behind it. It is worth reminding ourselves that evidence comes in two broad categories, evidence as it appears in court and evidence that you, as a forensic scientist, will find, analyse and include in your report. That is basically the physical material from the crime scene or samples from individuals. These very rarely get taken into court, although this does happen on occasion. So in respect of the forensic scene, what constitutes evidence? The answer is simple: anything. It is up to the scientist to package the information in such a way that it helps the court come to a conclusion, hopefully the correct one, without becoming bogged down in details of the methods of analysis. It is your job to provide a digest of the material in your written report. There are many aspects to handling evidence and the way in which it is analysed, but there are some principles which the court has every right to assume have been dealt with.

Forensic Science in Court: The Role of the Expert Witness   Wilson Wall
© 2009 W. J. Wall

The court is going to expect that data with which it is provided is going to be of use in the case; in the USA this is referred to as 'helpfulness'. The decision as to what will be taken to court will depend upon the counsel for the client, not the forensic scientist, but counsel will need to know about any tests that have been carried out and whether they produced a usable result, or not. It is also going to be assumed by the court that the method, no matter what it is, is sound and reliable and, in the case of new techniques, that the laboratory carrying out the test is adequately certified to take on the task. There should also be retained material wherever possible. Sometimes this may not be practical as the test uses all the collected evidence, but if there is material left over from testing, this should be kept as the other side of the case may like independent analysis of the material. Even after the evidence has been analysed and a report generated, the laboratory records, that is beyond just the report, should be available for scrutiny by other interested parties. This is especially important where reanalysis is no longer possible as it is effectively the 'working out' of the forensic scientist which demonstrates that the results are sound and can be relied upon. It should be remembered that if the proper procedures are not carried out in the analysis, even if the conclusions are unaltered, it is likely that the results will be challenged and the forensic evidence declared inadmissible.

Before looking at the broad categories of evidence as they apply to the courts (see also Figure 3.1) it is useful to look at the sort of practical quandary that a forensic scientist might find themselves in when expressing what is essentially their opinion regarding evidential value of data. The problem which arises with data generated from analysed material is the question of certainty. This is an area which will keep reappearing because it is central to the plausibility of the forensic scientist and the probity of their evidence. If a witness makes an assertion that two samples originated from the same place, whether that is a person in the case of body fluids, or paint from a vehicle, the statement made is one of practical certainty. When the analysis involves a probability database, a figure of likelihood can be produced, but that is generally difficult to interpret for the benefit of the court as the probability becomes larger. For every probability that is not equal to 1, there is a residual doubt, however small, that can be used by the cross-examining lawyer to advantage if the scientist makes a bold statement of certainty. On this basis alone it is important to be clear in your own mind what the probability is and what it means in probative value. There are few forensic systems in place that have been so

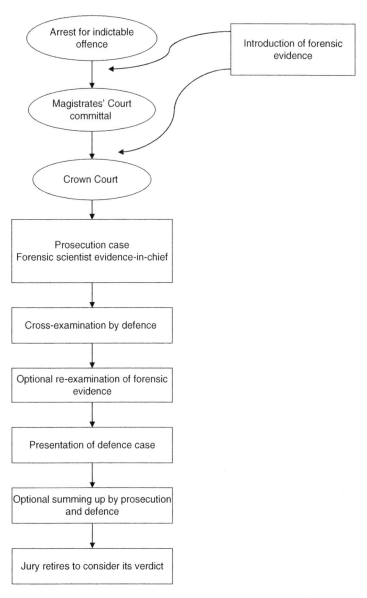

Figure 3.1   Flow of a criminal indictment through the court system with emphasis on the forensic scientist.

rigorously investigated in this respect as DNA analysis for the profiling of individuals. This is in contrast to fingerprint evidence that has been presented to courts for many years as a practical certainty, with no critical assessment of the data in the same way that DNA is assessed. This problem of expressing a probability in a meaningful way is dealt with in more detail in the chapter on statistics.

The expert can be put in a very difficult position if it is not clear what can and cannot be said. This may seem like an odd thing, but it is because there are different categories of evidence. Broadly these are evidence of fact, evidence of opinion and hearsay evidence. It can be easily seen that this also reflects the value which a court puts upon the evidence. It is obvious that evidence of fact is, or should be, incontrovertible; evidence of opinion is based on an interpretation of the facts and this interpretation is sometimes open to debate. It is here that forensic scientists and scientific experts can dispute within the court the meaning and interpretation of particular information. Hearsay evidence is not generally held in high esteem by courts and the weight given to hearsay evidence is a matter for the judge. This is a direct consequence of the nature of hearsay evidence. It is essentially second-hand information, such as an overheard comment, or evidence given by someone other than the originator of the information. There are many problems with hearsay evidence, some of which are due to the way in which courts in the UK operate. For example, witnesses are generally cross-examined in court by opposition lawyers, so written or spoken hearsay evidence associated with an individual not in court cannot be cross-examined. For this reason hearsay evidence is generally excluded, but there are exceptions to this situation. For example, a witness repeating what was heard said by another person, such as 'I am going to kill you', would not necessarily be considered hearsay as it indicated a direct intent to commit murder. Certain types of hearsay evidence are accepted, such as a confession of guilt, followed by silence at the following trial. Because of questions regarding the potential for false confessions, such confessions are only admissible if they have been made during a formal (recorded) interview while the accused was in custody. Other situations where hearsay evidence is acceptable involve such situations as a death-bed statement, the speaker not having any reason to lie and also being unable to testify in person.

With hearsay evidence it is important for the court to take into account a number of factors which may help in assessing its evidential value. The first, of course, is whether it really should be hearsay, or whether the person who originally said, or reported, the statement being used as hearsay could reasonably be expected to appear in person in court, which would change hearsay evidence to evidence of fact or opinion. An interesting, but difficult to test, situation that needs to be evaluated is whether the hearsay evidence originated at the same time as the event being investigated by the court. If the hearsay was not contemporaneous it would bring into question as to whether it was made up for ulterior reasons. This also impinges on the question as to whether any person involved in the evidence had any motive to conceal or misrepresent it, similarly whether the circumstance of the hearsay evidence would indicate that proper evaluation is not possible.

With the undoubted value of having a witness in court to give their own evidence it is possible, if the witness is available, for them to be called. This is specifically for civil cases where one side may use hearsay evidence, but not call the individual as a witness in court. Under these circumstances it is possible with the leave of the court for the opposing side to call the witness for cross-examination. This would normally only occur where the caller of the hearsay evidence does not want the witness to undergo cross-examination because they are a weak witness.

There is one restriction of hearsay evidence in civil cases which results in the evidence not being admitted. This is the situation where the witness has such mental or physical infirmity that understanding the process of the court would render them unsuitable as witnesses. Hearsay evidence can be tested in a number of ways in the absence of the witness, such as demonstrating that before or after the statement was made the witness contradicted part or all of the hearsay evidence. Hearsay evidence in both civil and criminal cases is fraught with difficulties for the court and both sides in the argument.

In criminal cases the burden of proof lays with the prosecution, who must provide a level of proof which is beyond reasonable doubt. This is different to civil cases where it is a balance of probability that one side or the other are wrong that is used to define the outcome.

Burden of proof in these cases is not confined to proving the prosecution case, but also to trying to discredit the defence evidence. The aim of all this for the court is to find out what really happened. As can be appreciated, sometimes it is not straightforward, as in the case of when only two people are involved and it might be seen as one word against another's. It is an unusual situation where a prosecution is pursued by a private individual, but it does happen in a surprisingly large number of cases and being a prosecution, regardless of the origin or perpetrator of the indictment, the standard and burden of proof remains exactly the same.

Pursuing a prosecution

It would be easy to assume that the Crown Prosecution Service has always had control of prosecutions in criminal cases and that it has been in existence since the rule of law became formalised, but this is not so. Prosecution of miscreants within society, by society, has a very long lineage, based upon the principle that it is essential to have proscribed activities to maintain a functioning society. So we generally find that murder, theft and other agreed unpleasant activities are not tolerated and therefore individuals perpetrating them are sought out and punished by society. This is a public assessment of crime, separate from civil cases, and allows any member of the public to bring a prosecution for a crime. The difference between a civil case and a criminal case is that in a criminal case the prosecutor does not need to have any personal interest in the case; in a civil case they do have to. Perhaps surprisingly, there are a relatively large number of private prosecutions, mostly by companies and institutions, both government and private, with a relatively small number being the responsibility of private individuals. In the Prosecution of Offences Act 1985 there is a section which allows for the High Court to deny a serial or malicious prosecutor from proceeding with a case, but other than this there are few controls on the individual from pursuing a private prosecution. If a private prosecution is started by an individual it is not possible for them to drop it at a whim, it must be followed through. Similarly, if a private prosecution is successful and sentence passed, the prerogative of pardon rests with the Crown alone, not the instigator of the case.

Sometimes it is possible that the case is too unlikely to proceed successfully for any of the involved parties, or may be seen as simply wasting the time of the court. In this case the attorney general can take the prosecution over with the intention of dropping it entirely, which the private individual who started the case cannot do.

As far as forensic scientists are concerned, many of the rules of evidence are not strictly relevant to their work, but some most definitely are. We can think of evidence as being of several types. For the forensic scientist one of the most important is appearing in court as a witness, either of fact or opinion. After that there are broadly two different types of evidence, documentary and hard evidence. Documentary evidence is more or less what it says: documents detailing events, or might be tape recordings. Whatever the nature of documentary evidence is, proving it to be authentic is paramount. This is one of the reasons why a clearly documented chain of custody for exhibits is of paramount importance. It is essential that the court has faith in the nature and origin of documentary evidence, especially if the documents themselves are particularly significant to the court. As far as the forensic scientist is concerned, the systems are generally already in place to maintain the chain of custody and should not be the subject of a shortcut. It is paramount that the chain of custody is reliable. This reliability is dependent upon a number of individuals and a number of methods. These include always signing and dating any bags which have been used for the collection of samples. The bags should be tamper proof: that is, they are incapable of being opened without destroying the seal of the bag. If the bag is opened for any reason, then when it is re-closed the closure should be signed and dated by the person who opened the bag. Although we generally think of this level of control being associated with real evidence, that is physical items of evidence, it is also very important when dealing with documentary evidence, especially when this includes material which could possibly be altered, or tampered with, such as recordings and paperwork if there is any doubt as to its validity or originality. When a piece of documentary evidence is produced by a third party to the case before the court, it may be necessary for the individual who produced it to appear as a witness to explain how they came to be in possession of it and what its provenance is. Again, this is unlikely to affect the professional forensic scientist because the chain of custody will be well established.

As was mentioned above, real evidence is made up of 'things' which might be of significance at the trial. These might be weapons, or possibly documents which contain the defendant's signature. In this latter case a piece of documentary evidence is transformed into a piece of real evidence if the document is of an incriminating nature, or an admission of guilt.

Although we can divide evidence into varying types, the question remains: what should we do with it? This may sound like a strange question, but remember that not all evidence needs to be, or will be, used in court. For example, a lawyer may decide that certain evidence will not help the case one way or the other and so should not be brought before the court. This is in part because the lawyers and the judge want a quick and robust case put before them without unnecessary complications and arguments that have little or no evidential significance. So do not be surprised if your forensic evidence is not used, which, if you are being honest and accurate in your analysis and state that the evidence is inconclusive, is the most likely outcome for your report.

Any evidence which is going to be used in the Crown Court has to be revealed to the other side. This is not so in the case of proceedings in the Magistrates' Court, where although it is not a stated requirement for one side to show the other evidence that will be used later, if the case is going to end up in the Crown Court, it is usual for both parties to reveal their evidence at the time of the magistrates' hearing. This is for the simple reason that it avoids one side or the other having to request an adjournment when the case is about to be heard at the Crown Court so that an expert can be appointed to go through the evidence. This obviously helps in the smooth running of the court so that proceedings can flow more naturally. After all, it is annoying for the jury as well as the judge, lawyers and the clerks that have to reschedule events because of late disclosure of evidence. Under certain circumstances it is rare, though not unknown, for non-disclosure of evidence then to be seen as important by one side or the other. When this happens, the non-disclosed evidence cannot be used, either as written or oral evidence from the scientist, without the expressed permission of the judge and the judge will only give leave for this if they think it is fair to do so.

Occasionally, and this has always been a surprise to me when it happens, a witness summons will turn up in the post. The witness is asked, more correctly demanded, to appear in court to give evidence. The witness is asked to confirm in writing that they will appear. This is where it can become tricky because if the witness does not reply, or says that they will not appear in court, then the lawyer asking for the person to appear as witness will write to the court stating that the witness either will not, or cannot, appear as a voluntary witness. At this point the court can issue a witness summons for the individual to appear. As a forensic scientist you are unlikely to be on the receiving end of this sort of summons, but as a colleague used to point out, one volunteer is worth 10 pressed men and the court knows this. Interestingly it is possible for a witness summons to be prepared for every witness and this might be so in particularly convoluted cases. Under these circumstances the forensic scientist, who will be scheduling their work to include appearances in court, will also receive a summons. It is part and parcel of the process of giving evidence in court. One thing about a witness summons which should not be ignored is that it is a very serious document. If, for whatever reason, you fail to attend the hearing after receiving the summons, there are a number of things that can happen. You may be arrested, you will definitely be brought to court and asked for an explanation, you may be fined and in extreme circumstances imprisoned. This apparently draconian power should not affect a competent scientist because what it does do is underline the power of the judiciary to find out the truth, as well as is possible, and if that means a witness to the great and the powerful, that is what will happen. Nobody is above the law when the police arrive and tell you that you are required at court.

Now, just as evidence can be described as falling into different categories, so too can witnesses. Broadly there are witnesses of fact, witnesses of opinion and professional witnesses. In general the professional witness is differentiated from forensic scientists by virtue of the method by which they are paid for appearing in court. A professional witness is not a witness who does it professionally, but a professional who is acting as a witness. A professional witness usually gives evidence of fact, the evidence having been seen or heard as a part of their everyday professional activities. Prime examples of this are the police who might be called to the crime scene and make notes which can then be turned into a statement. They are statements because, although professional witnesses can give some opinion, they are not generally, and should not generally, interpreting the evidence of fact which they are giving in their statement. This is in contrast to a forensic science report, which by its very nature may require interpretive opinion. Although evidence of fact generally requires cross-examination in court, a statement from a professional witness, if not disputed by either party, can be read out in court without the need either for the professional to be present, or for cross-examination.

There is an area called the ultimate issue rule, which is, as it implies, associated with the ultimate issue that the court has to decide upon. It is essential that the expert does not usurp the position of the court or jury in this, whether inadvertently or not. It is very easy, especially in civil cases, for the forensic scientist to slip into the position of advocate for the client; it is also easy in criminal cases for the forensic scientist inadvertently to direct the jury. This would be seen as taking on the position of the jury, which is simply not acceptable. A witness should never be asked a question as to the guilt or innocence of a person in court, it would be quite wrong for a lawyer to ask such a thing and if the judge did not stop the proceedings to admonish the advocate it would be incumbent upon the forensic scientist to declare an inability to make such a judgment. It should always be remembered that it is perfectly valid for a jury to ignore, or downgrade, the evidence of an expert or forensic scientist. The most likely reason for this is if the evidence is presented in such a way as to be too complicated; there are no concepts which someone familiar with their subject cannot make plain to a third party with a little practice. If, as often happens, a case comes to rest around a single point of evidence, it may be the forensic evidence which is pivotal. It is for the court to decide what weight to give to such material. It may be thought too much or too little by the forensic scientist, but it is for the jury to assess in light of the presentation by the scientist, not for the scientist to assess and then give an opinion.

It is not always easy to steer away from subjective opinion when giving evidence. This is especially so when it is a matter of mental health – psychological evidence as to an accused individual's condition regarding whether they are, or are not, fit to plead is just such a point. Insanity, in broad terms for the benefit of the court, can be thought of as a disease of the mind. This is where the fundamental problem can arise regarding a reductionist viewpoint or a more ethereal viewpoint as to what constitutes the mind, rather than the brain as an organic part of the person. Simply, is it possible for the mind to be diseased without the brain being diseased, even if that is a simple chemical imbalance? It is here that it becomes very easy for the forensic psychologist to step over the line of the ultimate rule because it is for the court to judge whether an individual is suffering from a disease of the mind, which is precisely what the psychologist is deciding in making a determination of insanity. Psychological evidence and psychiatric evidence have always attracted rigorous debate in court. It would not be overstating the case to say that they have been regularly attacked by lawyers and anyone else that has an opinion on the matter. The point comes down to whether the lines drawn up by the law regarding sanity and free will have anything to say regarding a medical diagnosis which is primarily made for treatment of the patient.

With psychological evidence, and with many other types of evidence which can appear in forensic situations, such as handwriting or some of the more obscure techniques employed like stylometry (see box below), it is not possible to generate meaningful rates of occurrence of specific aspects of the evidence. In the case of medical or psychological evidence this often takes the form of a descriptive syndrome. Although much misused as a word, a syndrome is a collection of elements that appear in a specific condition. It is then called a syndrome for diagnostic labelling purposes, but all the possible parts that can make up the syndrome do not have to be present for it to be described as such. Take, for example, Down's syndrome, which is easily recognised in most cases and was described as a syndrome by J. L. Down long before the cause of the condition was known. As it has been so well documented over the last 150 years, there is a long list of symptoms that can be associated with the condition. Some of them are highly suggestive of the syndrome, some of them occur less often, but what is certain is that the complete list does not appear in any one individual. So in a forensic situation where a mental state is being debated, the aspects of a patient's condition which to an untrained eye might seem important may well be irrelevant to the diagnosis, and so we come to rely upon experts for their opinions.

Stylometry

Stylometry can be part of the process of examining documents, along with the type of paper, the style of handwriting or the type of printer upon which they have been produced. Although it may be thought that a questioned document which is, say, a handwritten poison-pen could be disguised by the simple act of using print cut from commonly available documents such as newspapers, or printing them on an anonymous printer, much can be inferred from the use of words. Word usage in its simplest form would be the recognition of rare and unusual words that a known individual might use. A development of this technique can be used as a tool in the authentication of historical documents by analysis of the style of writing. This is stylometry. Questions of authenticity can be of great significance, as in the case of disputed authorship of works attributed to Homer, or in the published versions of plays by Shakespeare, the first folio edition having been published after his death. When questions of this type have been asked, it has usually been by individuals looking at the problem from an academic perspective, using a very subjective analysis. There are statistical methods which can be used to make this sort of style analysis, one of which is a cumulative sum graph, sometimes simply referred to as a cusum analysis.

As a forensic tool stylometry has many shortcomings and is not generally acceptable as evidence in court. This stems from the proponents of the technique, whether subjective or cloaked in the statistical technique of cusum analysis, being unable to demonstrate that it has any reliable background data which supports the claims made for it. Until such an evaluation has been made for stylometry it is best to stay well away from it as a forensic tool.

A traditional attitude in courts in the UK and many overseas courts is that witnesses and evidence of fact are the best evidence. This is certainly true in the case of primary documents, but as a principle the best evidence rule has been eroded. When it comes to a witness of fact giving first-hand testimony as to what was seen or heard, eye witness testimony has suffered due to the undeniable nature of eye witness accounts. This does not mean that evidence of fact can be disregarded. Several eye witness accounts might reinforce the overall picture of events. As a forensic scientist giving evidence of fact it is unlikely that you will be witness to the original events, but you will be a witness of both fact and opinion. Although identification evidence and eye witness accounts may be viewed as fallible, a witness of fact may be someone like a police officer who has made notes at the crime scene regarding the details of what was found. It is perfectly reasonable for a witness of fact to use written records made at the time, or immediately afterwards, to refresh their memory as to details and even to read out directly to the court. Such notes can be inspected by the other side. Now, just as it is important to keep track of who handled physical evidence and what tests were performed, it is also important to record times, places and dates when notes were made or procedures carried out. This will be dealt with in more detail in the chapter covering the written report. Interestingly, although a witness of fact is not generally allowed to sit in court during testimony of other witnesses, the forensic scientist may be required to because of the nature of their evidence in relation to the scientist for the other side. There are many and varied situations where witnesses of fact do not need to be in court, for example if they are dead, or if both parties have seen the written statement and no cross-examination is seen as necessary.

It is normal for a witness of fact to give oral evidence directly to the court, although in certain circumstances where there is no dispute regarding the evidence in a written report, it may just be read out instead. Things can get a little unclear here, because a witness of fact should only testify regarding what they heard or saw themselves, otherwise the evidence becomes hearsay. However, it has become commonplace now for forensic analysis of material to be carried out in one laboratory and reported from another, simply by taking the completed results and reporting them.

When it comes to scientific evidence the scientist will be giving evidence of both fact and opinion. Although this has been stated here before, it is worth repeating because your evidence of opinion must only be based on your evidence of facts and your understanding of them. Two types of facts can be represented here and are simply a matter of common sense: there are the facts which you will have observed yourself and there are the facts which you will have confidence in but have only been told them, either orally or in writing, as in the chemical composition of paint taken from a vehicle and analysed by a specialist who then passed the results on to another scientist. Under these circumstances the evidence, the data, still remains evidence of fact. It has been said that evidence produced by the testifying experts themselves will be looked on with most favour, but this is not necessarily so and reflects the changing manner and the changing level of complexity of modern scientific analysis. Usually a forensic scientist will not be pressed on this matter, although in some older court systems where modern forensic evidence of extreme complexity is still relatively rare, a forensic scientist may still come up against the belief that if they have not carried out the work which they are reporting it is somehow of less evidential value than if they had done the analysis themselves.

Forensic scientists and expert witnesses are able to give to the court opinions on the factual evidence because the court may not know, or be unaware, of the complex scientific basis of the results being presented. What it comes down to is that the court needs the help of expert opinion in understanding the matters put before the court, which may be scientific material of a new and novel kind, or, most commonly, details of white-collar crime where forensic accountants will be involved. It has been mooted in complicated fraud cases that the jury system should be removed because the explanations are so complicated that it is sometimes difficult, if not impossible, for a jury of non-experts to understand the proceedings put before the court. As yet this has not happened, but with financial transactions becoming international and electronic the movements of funds, both legal and illegal, are becoming ever-more difficult to trace and the sums involved ever larger. Giving an opinion as an expert is at the discretion of the court based on qualifications and experience. The more experience that you can bring to a case, the easier it will be for the court to accept your opinion, but possibly more important than that, the court will be able to understand it. This is not such an odd point: the more experience you have in your chosen area, the more you will gain the ability to put over complicated ideas to a lay audience, in this case the jury. Expertise which can be used in court covers anything that is slightly outside day-to-day knowledge.

Although forensic scientists are mainly associated with criminal trials, scientific expertise is increasingly being used in civil cases, but it is traditionally the criminal trial with which the scientist is associated. Giving evidence of opinion as a forensic scientist is a matter of taking the evidence of fact and producing an opinion on whether or not the defendant had anything to do with the criminal act, either directly or as an accomplice in some shape or form. For these reasons it is essential that the forensic scientist has access to all the details of the charges and especially the nature of the offence which resulted in the charges being made. If a scientist is appearing for the defence it is also important for the scientist to know what the lawyers have decided regarding the form of the defence. There is little point in the scientist attacking in their report an aspect of the case which is of no concern to the defendant's position or of interest to the court.

There are areas where great care should be exercised in the way in which evidence of opinion should be expressed. One aspect of this will be dealt with in more detail in the chapter covering statistical interpretation of data, but here I will just cover the language which may confuse the judge and jury, resulting in a difficult cross-examination.

The use of assumptions by a scientist in court should always be avoided. This may sound like common sense, but it is easy to jump to a conclusion and although this is a very human process, it falls to you to make sure you are not a party to it. This can be exemplified by a situation where an individual has glass splinters in the soles of their shoes which match the glass at a break-in. The glass matches, and here we are disregarding the statistical aspects for clarity of the model, so the assumption is that the individual was at the crime scene where, say, a window was broken to gain access. Other evidence may help to clarify this situation, as to whether the defendant was present or not. Other evidence is important because Locard's principle can become more important than it should be in light of new technologies. Locard's principle is basically stated along the lines that whenever an individual enters a room they will leave a trace behind them. Now, we should be clear on several ideas here, which as scientists we should be aware of. The first is that science moves on and the second is that dogmatic assertions are not necessarily correct. So now we have the situation of a broken window, giving access to premises for the purpose of a burglary, with an arrested individual having glass associated to the broken pane lodged in the sole of their shoe. A straightforward statement is that the glass came from the window, putting the defendant at the scene of the crime, even though they might have been walking innocently past the premises after the event.

Then we have more complicated situations, because planting of evidence and accidental presence of evidence can add a further complication to the position of the analysing scientist. It is a problem which every scientist should be aware of because it echoes the idea that association is not automatically causal. So, in a simple form, if people go to bed when it gets dark, it does not mean that people going to bed make it go dark. More complicatedly, what if a sample of DNA was found at the scene of a crime relating to a known individual? Unlike the glass sample, the DNA almost certainly came from the individual in question, but here again we have to look at the statistical chapter to be sure of the figures. So, given that the DNA sample came from an individual at the scene of the crime, how can we be sure that the sample was not moved there from a different place?

This argument has taken place in court. The defendant was charged as being an accomplice to the burglary of a public house. It was alleged that the defendant was acting as a lookout and smoked cigarettes, throwing the cigarette ends on the ground while he waited for his accomplices. A second, real, situation was along the same lines. Someone was brought to trial on the basis of a match between DNA found on the cigarette ends at the scene of the burglary and the DNA of the defendant. Again, we shall go into the details of the scientific analysis in a later chapter, but here we want to look at where expert opinion should stop. In both these cases it can be said by the forensic scientist that DNA (whatever the probability is) was found which matched the DNA profile of the accused. What the forensic scientist cannot say anything about at all is how the samples with the DNA got to the scene of the crime. The defence in the first case was that the defendant had been at the public house and had smoked a cigarette while there, in the car park, and this is what had been picked up and analysed, with a consequent match to his DNA profile from a previous misdemeanour. Now, under these circumstances, other evidence would be a far more powerful lever. The forensic value of the DNA match is simply that it demonstrates that a DNA profile matching an individual was found, but it tells us nothing else, such as why it was there. In a similar vein, in the second case the cigarette end with DNA was inside the burgled house. In this case there was an exceptionally sound alibi for the accused and it turned out that his 'friends' who carried out the burglary had taken one of his cigarettes and deliberately dropped it as incriminating evidence while carrying out the burglary. So the evidence of fact as presented by the forensic scientist is that a DNA profile was found which matched the accused – nothing more. The evidence of opinion is the interpretation of the evidence of fact in saying that the probability of finding a match by chance is $1/N$. Opinion must have a sound basis, which is where evidence of fact comes into the equation.

Forensic scientists and experts employed by one or the other side of an argument will generally write a report, which is different to the statements produced by witnesses of fact and professional witnesses by virtue of its containing an interpretation of the facts, an opinion. In the next chapter we shall look at the general requirements of writing a report. The report may be read out in court and the author may or may not be called to give oral evidence, as examination-in-chief or cross-examination. If the scientist is required to give oral evidence based on their report then the report can be taken into the witness box as long as it is not annotated. It may also be necessary to take any notes or specific workings that were made if questions arise of a complex nature that require more detailed information than that held in the report.

If we take evidence as the usual means of proving or disproving a case, or the facts at issue in a case, then the rules of evidence must also give some clear indication of what constitutes evidence. For a forensic scientist this may not be so straightforward as the science which the scientist would like to put to the court may outstrip the ability of the court to understand it. This is important because it is axiomatic that the party that brings a case, whether it is the Crown Prosecution Service in criminal cases or an individual in a civil case, must prove the validity of the case. This is a constant part of the dispute and if at the conclusion of the case the original charge or claim has not been proved, the case is lost. The forensic scientist is not partisan, so it is incumbent upon the scientist to be free and fair with material and data generated from whatever samples and tests have been used. If the other side of the case wants to see your laboratory notes, or visit the testing laboratory to audit the work which was carried out, it is not a personal attack on you or the testing laboratory, but a genuine attempt to find the truth as revealed by the data – not the truth of the case, as that is for the court to decide, but the truth of the information as presented to the court which will influence their final decision.

As we have noted elsewhere, trials are combative but cannot be conducted by ambush, so any evidence that is going to be used during the trial has to be revealed to both parties. If this includes a forensic report, produced by either the prosecution or defence, it has to be disclosed to the other side. Up until that point the report is privileged: that is, like all communications between the lawyer, the client and the writer of the report regarding the court case, civil or criminal, unless it is going to be used the information is privileged and does not have to be revealed to the other side. It sometimes transpires that a report emanating from one side or another is of no use as evidence, or may even be detrimental to a case, in which event it would not be used as evidence and therefore would not be required to be revealed to the opposing side. In the UK the Crown Court (Advanced Notice of Expert Evidence) Rules 1987 specifically lay out the position in stating that expert evidence to be relied on at trial must be revealed in advance so that there is no surprise evidence. All this refers to material specifically produced for the trial. Any records, reports or, in the case of fraud, accounts that were produced before litigation was considered do not have privileged document status and therefore, whether they are to be used as evidence or not, must be available to both parties. In criminal cases, where the burden of proof is on the prosecution, the duty of the prosecution to reveal unused documentation is stricter than for the defence because the defence have the right to keep unused or unfavourable evidence to themselves.

Part of the reason for privilege is that it is imperative that the client has confidence in their legal team and this is helped by knowing that nothing said will be passed on without the client's permission. The client can waive the right of privilege, but the solicitor cannot.

4

Appointment of Experts and the Written Report

In this chapter we shall look at the appointment of experts and what should go into a written report. The contents of a written report are generally universal because courts always want the same sort of information so that they can be sure of the *bona fides* of the person writing the report. The reason that these two, apparently, different subjects are put together is because they are actually very closely linked. The appointment of an expert in a criminal case in the UK used to be based on a simple premise, which was that the prosecution took their expert from the Forensic Science Service, more by a lottery system than anything else. The Crown Prosecution Service (CPS) is the government unit which decides whether a case, any case, should be pursued through the courts as a prosecution. The CPS does not generally become involved in civil cases. This is a very important point. It is sometimes thought that the police decide when an individual is prosecuted. This is not so in any civilisation where the judiciary is separate from the state.

The police may arrest an individual, but whether the individual is brought before the court is a matter for the CPS to decide. Sometimes it appears that strange decisions are made, but the CPS is privy to a great deal of information and its decision should be respected. It is also possible for an individual, or group of individuals, to take out a private prosecution. This is a complex and expensive procedure. A private prosecution is a prosecution carried out by a private individual or an organisation. There are several such situations and

Forensic Science in Court: The Role of the Expert Witness   Wilson Wall
© 2009 W. J. Wall

they tend to be at the discretion of the court and CPS as to whether they are allowed to proceed. The reasons for stopping a private prosecution tend to be based on whether the CPS believes that further evidence will become available to pursue a Crown prosecution.

Centralised prosecutions

There has been a long tradition of private prosecutions, and in general terms there are few restraints on an individual from starting such proceedings (see the box in Chapter 3), but generally prosecutions now arise from a central origin. The way in which prosecutions are instigated can be seen to have originated in the historical past with the rise of centralised government and control of production. This was inevitably associated with the Industrial Revolution and the slow rise of an urban population moving away from small rural communities towards large conurbations where the individual had less regard for their neighbours as cities became dormitories for large numbers of workers with no personal relationship to each other. While this massive social change was taking place in the eighteenth century, two major shortcomings of what had until then been a perfectly adequate system became apparent. The first was that the use of a magistrate system for control of social order was not going to work and the second was that there was no professional police force. When towns and villages were small the local populace could be generally relied upon to undertake law enforcement, but at that time it was usually of direct consequence to them. By the time when towns were becoming anonymous cities the idea of a private individual bringing a criminal case against someone else was not so popular, especially as costs had to be covered by the prosecutor. By the second half of the century provision was made for payment of prosecutions by the state, but this was a relatively small amount. It did not take long for the control of criminal activity to move to what we would now think of as vigilantes. These prosecution societies as they were called were groups of private individuals who set up systems of watchmen and funded private prosecutions of those apprehended. Although there were civil police forces being formed by the time when Queen Victoria was crowned in 1837, they had no statutory ability to prosecute, so prosecutions by the police were carried out in a private capacity. There were several attempts to set up a single agency to be responsible for prosecutions and the office of Director of Public Prosecutions became established in 1879, though in a very limited capacity rather than a routine pursuer of justice. On this basis local police forces and, usually, local solicitors undertook prosecutions unless they were of particular public interest. It was not until the Prosecution of Offenders Act 1985 that the entire process was centralised with the introduction of the CPS to oversee and direct criminal prosecutions in the UK.

We can see from this that a government forensic scientist will generally be instructed by the CPS to carry out an analysis of the material which has been brought into the laboratory. While in the past analysis was carried out by the agents of the CPS in the form of the Forensic Science Service, this no longer holds true. Commercial companies can now bid for contracts which enable them, within tight government guidelines, to carry out analysis which the CPS will then take into court. Similarly it is no longer just the Forensic Science Service that is allowed to add names and profiles to the national DNA database.

When it comes to the appointment of forensic scientists, or scientific experts, the process can be quite long winded and involve what is, in effect, a chain of people. The process is broadly similar for either a civil or criminal case. In a criminal case a solicitor will be instructed by a defendant with respect to the charges being laid against them. The solicitor will look to the possibility of appointing a barrister for the defence, who, in turn, will prepare an opinion based upon the statements of those involved and any forensic reports which are relevant. If the defence team think it appropriate to appoint an expert they will most likely go with an expert they already know, but there are several registers of expert witnesses which cover virtually every scientific discipline. Once an expert has been located who specialises in that particular area of work, a written letter of instruction is issued, with the bare bones of the charges laid out. When it has been agreed to proceed with the work, the scientist should receive all of the relevant documents and reports.

As with all such consultations it starts with the review of evidence, as produced by the prosecution, which will be in the form of a forensic report detailing the relevant findings and interpretive opinion of the facts. The final stage will be the production of a report for the instructing solicitor. Whether it is used in court is a decision made by the legal team, not by the forensic scientist or independent expert. It should be noted here that any expert evidence in the form of a report can only be put as evidence with the court's permission. So as a forensic scientist you may be asked to prepare a report, generally for the prosecution, but if you are asked to prepare a report as an independent expert, generally for the defence, you should make sure that you have a letter of instruction, clear and concise, from your instructing solicitor, because that is the point when you will know that the court is prepared, if necessary, to accept your report as evidence. This is even more important in civil cases where an argument might arise which revolves around a specific point of a scientific or technical matter. Do not be tempted to address questions of law – that is neither your remit nor your area of expertise. Always confine yourself to what you know and what you can defend in cross-examination.

In civil cases it may be that the report is an adequate document and giving oral evidence will not be required, but there is always the possibility that a cross-examination based on the report will take place. It is at this point where it is necessary for the expert witness to be able to demonstrate that they have sufficient up-to-date knowledge to work at the cutting edge of a field as an expert. Not every jobbing scientist can be described as an expert, there is more to it than that. Just knowing and working in the subject are not the same as being *peritus*. It should be emphasised that courts are there to find the truth; they want you to do the very best you can, to explain difficult topics clearly and fluently. The court is not the cross-examining barristers, it is the group of people that form the jury in criminal cases and are guided by the judge, or in civil cases by a panel of judges. No matter what, the judge is arbiter and if things do become difficult you can always ask the judge to request the cross-examination by the barrister to be moderated in tone.

It is now within the ability of courts in the UK to do something which caused a great deal of consternation when it was first mooted as a possibility: that is, appoint a joint expert. Now this is, or was, a difficult concept in the UK because of the adversarial nature of the manner in which the court procedure works. It was almost inconceivable that an expert witness, whether an independent person or one attached to the Forensic Science Service, could possibly act for both sides in an argument. But consider what we have described before and will describe in future chapters – you are not partisan, you help the court come to the right conclusion. Sometimes things may go awry, but you do the best you can. This means that you report your results, provide conclusions and help the court. If you are for one moment seen as subjective rather than objective the whole basis of a single joint expert disappears. It should not be such a surprise that single joint experts are appointed by a court – it does, after all, have a long and noble tradition in another arena of conflict, namely the playing field. It is here that we see for the first time what is paramount in the court room. State the facts, give your opinion, where required, and hold true to the result. Do not, ever, take a partisan stance. It is this growing belief in the integrity of the forensic scientist that has allowed, probably grudgingly, acceptance of the concept of the single joint expert. Even so, it has caused some argument (see box below).

Saunder v. Birmingham City Council EAT 21/5/08

An attempt was made to overturn the decision of an employment tribunal on the grounds that the evidence of an expert should not have been accepted because of apparent bias. The court had directed that a single joint expert should be appointed, since no agreement was reached between the parties regarding an expert in the case, so the court appointed one from the list supplied by the council. The appellant (Saunder) tried to introduce evidence from two further experts. This was not received well by the court and the Court of Appeal held that the tribunal was correct in this case in refusing to disallow the evidence of the joint expert, but that the appellant should have been able to call his own expert. Any suggestion of bias should have been investigated in cross-examination.

It should be said that the single joint expert only works in civil cases, but that is not to say that the adversarial system might not take the notion on board. The appointment of a single joint expert is an interesting process, simply because the two parties have to agree to the individual involved. Now this, of course, is going to cause friction by its very nature, but the court cannot impose a single joint expert on the two parties. What the judge can do is prepare a list from suggestions by the two parties, or, rather more obscurely, direct that the expert is selected in a way that the court directs. Costs are important to the court and giving experts an open market has been seen as unproductive, so it is always within the ability of the court to restrict the use of experts. If the evidence is valid it will be heard; it is only when the arguments hinge on a minor detail that proceedings with regard to the expert witness, or forensic scientist, may be halted by the court.

The idea of the single joint expert tends to be associated with civil actions, not criminal investigations which often end up with each side appointing their own experts. In cases where a lot of expert evidence is to be used and court costs could get out of hand, this is where it is felt that a single joint expert could be used. In such cases the reliability and non-partisan nature of the appointed expert must be understood and accepted by all parties. It on this basis that Civil Procedure Rules 1998 primarily states that the court must give permission for an expert to be called.

When it comes to the written report, the expert is expected to maintain impartiality. The report should help the lawyers prepare their case and help the court understand difficult points. The investigator who then goes on to write the report might easily see relevant details to the case, but only if they have been given a detailed brief as to the case, be it civil or criminal. It is essential for the forensic scientist to be fully briefed as to the details of a case. There is little or no point in a forensic report containing an immense amount of detail which is simply not relevant to the case. This will at the very least lose favour with the court and at its worst result in the detail of a scientific finding which is pivotal to understanding the case being lost under a mountain of irrelevant facts.

In criminal cases the report should cover every salient aspect of the analysis that was carried out, including any shortfalls or inadequacies in the samples provided or the results as they are presented. This is not a case of owning up to mistakes so much as pointing out any limitations in the results which have been generated. If this is not done by you, the author of the report, it most certainly will be done during cross-examination, which will undermine any value that your evidence holds. It is particularly important to realise that it will not be possible in a report to hide or ignore adverse results. This may be inadvertent or accidental, but it will almost certainly be spotted by either your counsel or counsel for the other side and will certainly be spotted if the subject is of a technical complexity that is beyond the easy ability of counsel to understand such that they instruct their own expert to review the report and possibly the original evidence as well. If there is a case for another review of the evidence then another report will be produced and, just as the original forensic science report is shared with the other side of the case if there is anything to be used in court, the new report will be shared in the opposite direction if it contradicts the original report and will be used in court. It is essential that this exchange of ideas and interpretations of the forensic data takes place before court proceedings commence. If it were left to the point where the case went to court before these reviews of data and reports took place, it would unnecessarily increase the time which the case took in court for what may turn out to be trivial reasons. Complaints about reports, from one side or another, are frequently based around the way in which conclusions are expressed. This is because, while it may seem quite acceptable to be a little overenthusiastic in interpreting the probability of an event to make a point, it simply is not. On the contrary, it is far better to err on the conservative side when interpreting results so that no one can claim you are biased in your interpretation.

Once the reports have been served on the various parties involved in the case, the report of the forensic scientists may be used in criminal trials as a section 9 statement. This saves the scientist a lot of time as it means that, since there are no objections to the content from either side, it can be read out in court without the author of the report being present. Under these circumstances the judge and jury will have copies of the report which is to be read out: if it is going to be the subject of a cross-examination, the jury will need a copy of the report to make the proceedings easier to follow and the judge will need a copy to make notes of salient points.

Interestingly, it is generally thought that about 95% of civil cases, such as building boundaries, civil trespass and other non-criminal actions, are concluded without ever having to go to court. These cases which are sorted out without the intervention of a court are very often solved on the basis of a report prepared by an expert in a particular field. If the report is both authoritative and well prepared it can have a considerable influence on the final outcome. The standard of preparation is of vital importance, because although it may not seem sensible to make decisions based on arbitrary factors such as appearance, they will influence the opinion of the reader. It is of little use to you or your instructing lawyer if your report has its most important point, the one which can make a difference to the outcome of the case, swamped by bad grammar and poor spelling. Make the report clear and easy to read – the less contentious the content, the less likely you are going to have to defend the contents during cross-examination. Making the report clear and straightforward can best be done by always remembering that the majority of the people reading it will not have your level of technical expertise in the subject on which you are writing. Keep it simple and explain any terms which involve specialist knowledge. There is nothing wrong in attaching an appendix to a report which outlines the scientific and technical background to the test if this will help the lawyers and the court understand the important part of the information in the body of the report, but, again, it is essential to keep this sort of background material short, to the point and understandable. You are not demonstrating the depth of your knowledge – that is understood from the very fact that you are writing the report in the first place.

While in criminal cases the instructions as to which test type is required may be clearly stated, or obvious from the nature of the sample which has been forwarded to the laboratory, it is always worthwhile checking that you are not making an incorrect assumption. In the situation where you are instructed in a civil matter, the position may be far from clear as to what exactly the dispute is about, so always ask for details of the case from your instructing solicitor.

Whenever a report is produced it only needs to be disclosed to the other party in the case if it is to be used in court, so preliminary reports which may carry considerable additional material for the benefit of your instructing solicitor will not be shown to the other party. When you produce a final report it will be seen by a number of people, many of whom in civil cases will have an axe to grind as they will intrinsically think they are right. Avoid the contentious, explain exactly how you came to your conclusions and never stray out of your area of expertise.

There are a few indispensable items that go in a report, as follows.

On the first page your name and title. Then, beneath that, your occupation and your work address. You can enter here the instructing solicitor and the name of the case. Then it is normal to put in a statement to the effect that you realise that you owe a duty to the report and you have not put anything into the report which you know to be incorrect as this may result in a charge of perjury. Include a brief summary of your qualifications, from first degree onwards, but avoid mentioning junior qualifications. Also briefly say for how long you have been working in the field.

Don't forget to state how many pages there are in the total report, including appendices, and number every page next to the report date. Every page should be signed.

The second page should contain the report's contents. Do not be tempted to truncate the contents. All relevant sections of the report should be included in the contents, even if a section only constitutes a subheading and a single sentence. Paragraph numbers can also be used, but this may be a little excessive. Detailed contents are important because they speed up navigating around a report, especially if it is a long piece of work. Although the contents are at the front of the report it is self-evident that they should be the last thing produced.

On a very practical note, the report should be on good-quality paper and there should be enough copies for the protagonist lawyers and the judge, so it wise to check who is going to want copies so that you can print off enough of them. This can be a laborious activity, because every one has to have every page signed. Do not be tempted to have over-elaborate binding as it is quite likely that the report will be handed around and photocopied; as long as it is on good-quality paper it should not get too scuffed, but if it is solidly bound the photocopying process can make it all look very tatty.

Within the body of the text do remember to use lots of relevant headings for ease of navigation around the report. When the scientist gives evidence and is cross-examined, the lawyers and the judge will be making notes and they need space to do so on your report, so use double line spacing and have wide margins, anything up to 5 cm, either side. This may appear to make the body of the text narrow, but it is useful for the court. Lawyers will often put reports down in court onto a lectern, or bench top, from which they will want to read it without holding it too close and losing eye contact with the witness, so use a relatively large type face – 12pt is fine.

Two last remaining practical points: check spelling and grammar. There are lots of books available which direct the writer towards correct usage.

As a guide there is one thing about reports which can be stated with some certainty: every society, club and group of individuals believe that they have a model report format. Unfortunately, all of these reports bear a similarity to a phrase attributed to Sir Alec Issigonis, 'A camel is a horse designed by a committee.' They attempt to be a catch-all description of a report. Some aspects of the written report are common to many of these model reports, and these are broadly described below. One aspect that causes much concern is the declaration which should be at the beginning of the report. Some suggested wording amounts to a small essay, but all that is required is a statement to the effect that you have made an honest and impartial assessment of the evidence as presented to you for analysis. Anything more than this becomes tautological.

Front page:	Report on the [type] evidence in the case of [plaintiff/accused]
	Report prepared for [name and address of instructing authority]
	Report prepared by [your name, title and address]
	Report dated [day of printing]
	[Declaration of the validity of the report and the number of pages, all numbered and signed]
Second page:	Contents [lots of headings and subheadings for ease of navigation]
Body of text:	Introduction

            Tests and results

            Conclusions [bullet points are useful here for easy referencing]

Appendix: Technical details that require further clarification

Every page at the bottom should state it is part of the report of x pages, and should be signed.

5

The Expert Forensic Scientist in Court

There are two parts to this, the first is what you need to do before you arrive in court and the second is what you need to do when you have arrived in court. This second part also includes what you are going to be expected to do when you are in court, assuming that your report has been written and you are required to appear in court, which is by no means certain. In criminal cases, for example, unless there is a dispute between the scientists working for the prosecution and defence in the interpretation of the data, of whatever sort it is, you may not be asked to appear in court. The point I am making here is that not every case will require your presence in court, but if you are required to appear it is well to be as thoroughly prepared as it is possible to be.

If you are required to appear, hopefully you will be given adequate warning of when the court case is going to take place. Something to be remembered is that a forensic scientist will often be asked to appear in court at the other end of the country because, while forensic analysis facilities are often centralised, courts are not. This, of course, can add to the levels of stress which you may feel about going to court, so always organise your travel well in advance and write down exactly what your road, rail or flight route is going to be. Do not try to remember it, write it down. Having been given adequate warning of the date of the court case and having organised the travel, there should be plenty of time for getting together all the necessary documentation that you should

Forensic Science in Court: The Role of the Expert Witness Wilson Wall
© 2009 W. J. Wall

take. This documentation can be quite considerable: the more complicated the case, the more there will be. In criminal cases the more defendants there are, the more material there will be, not just because of duplication but also because the charges might not be the same for each individual.

Start by gathering all the evidence that you have access to – even material about which you could not be expected to answer questions is worth keeping with you. This bundle will include your report and also any photographs, graphs, documents from the other side of the case, whether it is a criminal or civil case, and any visual aids which you might require to explain difficult ideas or situations. If you do need visual aids which require material or equipment that is not readily portable, let the lawyers know as soon as possible. It should be remembered that, except for very simple systems, if visual aids go wrong it will reflect on your credibility, so unless you are certain as to how they work and can practise with them, which is unlikely, or there is a technician there to help you, they are best avoided. Once you have all the documentation to hand, put it into a logical order and reread your own report to become so familiar with it that you broadly know what is on every page. This may sound like unnecessary advice, but it is surprising how often people become complacent about their own work, forgetting that, during the occasion of cross-examination, having to thumb through your own report when giving evidence to find the relevant part does not give a good impression. So make sure your report is paginated in the same way as the reports that both the defence and prosecution have in front of them. This is important because, if there is a point in your report on which you are being specifically cross-examined, it will come in the form of 'on page xx of your report you state that. . .'. It is also worth making sure that your bundle of documents provided by your lawyer also is in page order and divided into sections. If the bundle is supplied in one lot by your instructing lawyer the entire file will often be sequentially paginated and it is worth keeping it in that form.

A lot of the material, especially in criminal cases, will not be directly relevant to your part in the case, but it is worth making an effort to see where the case is going so that you will not be taken by surprise. Doing this review well in advance of the commencement of the case is useful because, although you may have a broad idea from your counsel as to when you will be called, this may only be in terms of the rough order of proceedings, so it could easily be plus or minus a day. You do not want to be taken by surprise when you find yourself suddenly called to give evidence.

Once the files are sorted out a very important aspect of your pre-court activity is to identify the strengths and weaknesses of your case. This is more so in civil cases where putting the case cogently and fluently by your lawyer will depend on your level of clarity when dealing with them. Remember that since you will have been given copies of all the documents which the other side is going to rely on in court, you should also assess the strength and weaknesses of their case. This preparation is crucial. The opposing lawyer will try to expose the weaknesses in your report, as your lawyer will try to expose the weaknesses in their report. Try to play to your strengths: the more facts you have at your fingertips, the less likely it is that your opinion based on those facts will be disputed or disregarded. Be prepared for the questions you will most likely be asked so that you are not caught out. This preparation will also help in another way – confidence. If you are confident in the layout of your report you will be much surer of yourself when confronted with a lawyer asking questions which in themselves can be quite difficult to understand.

Something which many forensic scientists in their first forays into court forget, unless reminded by a colleague, is that your lawyer will ask about such things as qualifications and possibly publications, if these are relevant. If you can, it is best to commit these to memory. If you are asked about them it will usually be in a preamble to the evidence-in-chief and it should be with your prior agreement. Sometimes counsel might be pressed for time or just forget to mention that they intend to do this, but your instructing lawyer will have passed on any CV which you have given them, so do not be surprised if you are asked anyway. These are simply remembered, but, again, if you are not ready for the question it can go out of your head. Qualifications are such things as degrees, where awarded and the year, followed by the number of publications which are relevant. Details of publications are not necessary. When preparing a brief synopsis of your area of expertise, keep it short and keep it relevant – it is not a job interview, it is to ascertain your professional standing. So think of ways to describe your area of expertise; being overly modest will not do your credibility any good and neither will bravado. It is worth rehearsing this with a colleague if possible. There is no point in being coy about this, because when you go to court you may have to do it in front of an invited audience of complete strangers. Start by practising in front of a mirror, listen to how you sound and look at your body language, which can tell both the judge and jury a great deal about you, nearly as much as the words that you speak. Aim for an image of reliability, honesty and willingness to help. Too much detail can cloud the issue and may hide the important bits: for example, there is no point in my saying that I was editor of a botanical journal unless plant remains have been involved in the case; the court might hear that and miss the next bit about the ground-breaking work I had done on the subject under dispute.

Once you have organized the paperwork and, hopefully, yourself, make a list of all the things that you are going to take to court with you. This does not just mean the documents to be taken but all sorts of other items which will be necessary, or even just potentially useful. Such items may include, for example, pens, paper, a comb, a watch and so on. Pens and paper are essential because you may have to help out your lawyer with notes and guidance on questions which need to be asked. If you use a fountain pen make sure it is full of ink. There is nothing more irritating than having to borrow a pen once you are in court. Now, because the day of the trial that requires your presence is going to be a busy one for you, plan in advance what you are going to wear. This may sound strange, but it is worth doing this simply so that you do not have to think about it on the first day of the trial. If you consider what the solicitors and barristers wear, sober and smart, you will not want to stand out, more fit in, so do think in advance about what you are going to wear and avoid strident colours and loud stripes and definitely no clown shoes. Sometimes it is advised that men should wear 'sober' ties, but this does not mean dull (membership ties can be bright and cheerful and are ideal), just bear in mind that a tie with a cartoon character on it may detract from what you are saying and on balance is best avoided.

Speak to your lawyer regarding the expected duration of the trial and whether you will be required, or your lawyer would like you, to be there on days when you will not actually be giving evidence. This is quite likely, especially if the trial is highly technical in content. Even if the case is straightforward, or the forensic evidence or its interpretation is in dispute, you will need to hear the evidence of your opposite number so that you have a clear idea of the questions you will have to field when you give your evidence. It is also important to find out what the estimated duration of the trial is going to be. With straightforward criminal trials, such as assaults, estimates tend to be reliable and although proceedings may depend upon your report, even the morning or afternoon during which you will be required to give evidence can be accurately calculated. With civil cases these estimates can be far more difficult to calculate, as can complicated criminal trials where you may even be recalled later to give evidence again. One area where criminal trials can drag on for long periods is cases of fraud. These can be particularly difficult to unravel and involve an inordinate length of time and highly specialised skills, so time in court is difficult to estimate. Whichever type of case you are being asked to look into, give yourself far more time in your diary than the estimate you were given by your lawyer. One of the reasons why the time schedule of the court can slip is adjournments. These crop up for all manner of reasons and tend to be unpredictable. Similarly, tell your lawyer well in advance about dates when you are unable to appear; this may be for a number of reasons, such as a previously arranged court case or simply going on holiday. If sufficient notice is given the dates can be easily rearranged. Organising the appearance of so many people in one place at the same time is a daunting task for the clerk of the court and everyone involved, but it all seems to work.

As for getting to the court itself, preparation is important for your own peace of mind. Find out well in advance where the court is situated, which is nearly always centrally within a town, and how you are going to get there. Because of the way in which the courts and forensic science laboratories are positioned it is unlikely that a court will be local to you, so it is worth finding out whether it is a train ride or an air flight away. If you are travelling by car try to locate the nearest car park. Some courts do have their own car parks, but you might need to reserve a space. If it is possible, try to visit the court before the trial so that you know where it is specifically and, just as important, especially when driving, how to navigate around the town to find it. One-way systems can make what appears to be a simple journey quite complicated if you are not ready for them, and arriving late and flustered due to traffic or the road system is not a good idea, so always take a local map and always give yourself plenty of extra time for the journey. If you are arriving in a strange town, either by car or by train, and you do get lost the easiest thing to do is ask a police officer – they should all know where the court is and the best way of getting there, although it may not always be easy to find one. It can be useful to have access to a satnav system if you are driving, but remember that one-way systems can confound them.

Some courts are laid out in a haphazard fashion, so arrange with your lawyer an appropriate meeting point in the court building. You should be able to meet your solicitor easily enough because you will have dealt with them directly. On the other hand, you may not have met counsel before the court appearance, so you need to rely upon your solicitor to guide you to the appropriate barrister. However it is done, plan it beforehand and be clear in your mind where and when you are expected; this will be one less thing to bother about on the day.

Taking the strain out of court

Visits to specific courts can be intermittent and to some courts extremely rare. It is also true that although some barristers tend to specialise in specific areas, or types of crimes (perhaps that should be types of criminal prosecutions), you will be unlikely to see the same barrister from one year to the next. With solicitors the case can be even more extreme, for many solicitors may only see a criminal case in the Crown Court once in several years, so the chance of dealing with a solicitor more than once is even more unlikely. Some solicitors do have practices which specialise in criminal work, so these will appear rather more frequently as instructing solicitors.

With this in mind there is a useful notebook which you could produce. This is best divided up into three sections: courts, solicitors and barristers. With increasing visits to different courts and dealing with different solicitors and barristers, keeping a record of each one will help later on if, say, a year after your first visit to a court you are asked to go back again. The notebook can contain such things as the best way of getting to court, how long it takes and the layout of the building, including details such as toilets and catering facilities. This will enable you to find out quickly the details of the court and any of its quirks which you noticed on previous visits. This level of detail also applies to instructing lawyers and counsel, how they like to be addressed, any particular quirks (and some definitely have quirks), as well as any other details that help you get to court on time and in the right frame of mind.

In terms of preparation it is never too early to start practising being in court. If you have managed to visit the court in advance then try visualising yourself in that precise location. Try to develop a method of relaxation that you can use on the day – the more relaxed and confident you are, the better you will come over to the court when you give evidence. A note is in order here about 'the court': although it is generally thought of as the building and by implication the people present in it, strictly it is where the court sits and this can be anywhere. If an important witness, or even the accused, is incapable of getting to the court, perhaps through illness, the court can sit wherever it is deemed suitable.

The day, or evening, before you go to court, take one last look at your case notes and make sure they are in order. It is also worth checking with your solicitor that the case has not been adjourned and that someone has forgotten to inform you – these things do happen. Adjournments can be for any number of reasons, from problems with the jury to an inability of a witness to get to court through illness.

When you arrive at court you should have plenty of time to orientate yourself within the building; this is particularly valuable if it is your first visit to that particular building. One of the first things to do is locate the toilets and where you can get refreshments. Locating the toilets is important because that will be just about the only place in the building, other than the barristers' robing room, with a mirror. It is not so that you can preen yourself, but so that you can make sure you are presentable after your journey, especially if you have just come through high winds and rain. Before you make contact with your lawyers, locate the court and the time at which the case commences, also listen for announcements which may tell you that the case has been moved to another court, which is unlikely, or the case is ready to start. When you are inside the court, the proceedings can appear a little formal and positively odd if you are not used to them, but as we have seen in Chapter 1 the legal system has developed over many centuries and for all its foibles it retains a determination to get to the bottom of a case.

One of the first questions which you should ask your lawyers is who you can and cannot speak to. Generally you should not speak to other witnesses and you should never discuss the case with anyone other than your lawyers and the co-workers who might have helped with the forensic analysis. So if you are in any doubt as to whom you can speak, don't. Although witnesses of fact are generally excluded from the court until their testimony is specifically required, you can usually sit in on the whole proceedings if you want to. This can be quite useful to get a feel for the case and in some circumstances it can be quite entertaining.

Judges, barristers and solicitors

In the UK there are approximately 100,000 solicitors with current practising certificates. They take their name from their early situation of soliciting in areas where they were not recognised as advocates, like barristers, to try to speed up the actions of court officials. A solicitor became a generic title for an individual who organised and helped the advocates in their actions. It was only in the first half of the nineteenth century that soliciting could be said to have become a

(continued)

profession in its own right with the setting up of a governing society with a royal charter.

In contrast to the large number of solicitors there are only about 12,000 barristers in practice. These are the advocates who will take work provided by a solicitor, prepare a detailed appraisal of the case and flag up any additional work that needs to be done in preparation for the action in court.

All of the judges at every rank in the UK number approximately 3,800. All appointed judges are now required to retire at the age of 70. This was not always so and some have presided over cases in their eighties and nineties, although this has always been regarded as unusual.

The general layout of most courts means that when not giving evidence you will be sitting behind your barrister with the solicitor next to you. The judge is in front facing the court and the jury on your left, witness box on the right (Figure 5.1). In most jurisdictions the barrister is not allowed to move around the court while conducting the examination of witnesses and the barrister is provided with a lectern to support any of their notes and materials while they are standing and examining the witness.

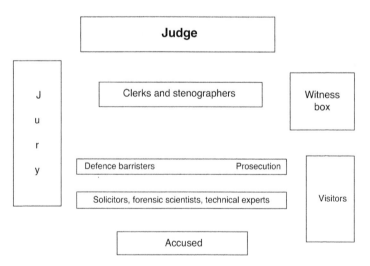

Figure 5.1 General layout of a modern Crown or County Court in the UK. This is a common plan now frequently copied around the world in new buildings, although in some overseas jurisdictions juries are not a normal part of the court.

This arrangement of sitting behind counsel, with or without the instructing solicitor, allows you to pass notes to your barrister to help clarify various points. In highly technical issues this may even include helping to direct the way in which questioning should go to clarify specific points which are in dispute. This process of helping to direct questioning is really quite common as it should be remembered that you are the expert, it is why you are there. The barrister, on the other hand, is the advocate, so needs your assistance to examine the case as presented by the opposing side. If you do find yourself doing this, it is as well to make sure you have enough pieces of paper to cover most eventualities. Write your comments and questions on clean paper, not A4, as this is too big, rather a quarter of this (A6) which should be more than enough. Unless there is a lot of information to pass over, keep the note short and to the point. Write in block capital letters so that the barrister can read it at a glance while it is flat on the bench. As with all such documents it is well to put a date on it, simply so that it does not get mixed up with another case or the same case on a different day.

Once inside the court the layout becomes obvious and varies very little between senior courts. The judge sits at one end on a raised area, and in front of the judge there will be the bench for the barristers, the prosecution and defence sharing the bench, behind them comes the solicitors for each party and any forensic scientists or experts as are required. Between the judge and the barristers there is an area occupied by the court officials and clerks.

Hearsay and the expert

Using the Civil Evidence Act 1995, hearsay can be defined as a statement made otherwise than by a person while giving oral evidence in the proceedings. Put more simply, hearsay can be a reported conversation by the witness, 'I was told that. . .', or even as second hand when the witness recounts what they were assured another person had said. The exact distance between the witness and the origin of the evidence may make it difficult for the court in civil cases to assess the value of the hearsay evidence. In criminal cases the situation is slightly different as there is no equivalent to the Civil Evidence Act 1995.

For the forensic scientist, it is important to remember that everything you do and carry out is based on the scientific investigations of others. It is for this

(continued)

reason that hearsay does not generally apply to forensic evidence, as long as it is based on sound science. For example, it would be unrealistic for every case involving DNA analysis to be carried out and the statistical analysis started from scratch each time, with a new frequency database being prepared and the logical derivations produced from first principles. We have to accept that some things with which we may not be personally familiar are sound and reliable.

A case where this idea of forensic evidence being hearsay was tested can be found in *R. v. Abadom* [1983] 1 All ER 364. This revolved around the charge of robbery being backed up by the statistical analysis of shards of glass found in the sole of the shoe of the accused being of a type rarely found. The statistic of frequency was challenged at appeal on the basis that the prosecution forensic scientist had no personal knowledge of how the statistics were arrived at – effectively implying that this was inadmissible hearsay evidence. This was dismissed by the Court of Appeal and the conviction stood.

The most important thing for you will be the witness box and how you deal with your evidence-in-chief and any cross-examination that takes place. As a piece of furniture the witness box is not particularly aesthetic, more functional. It is usually square and nearly always slightly raised. Although a witness would normally stand while giving evidence, if there is any infirmity or other reason that standing is not desirable or comfortable, a chair can be provided. The witness box is generally to one side and usually to the left of the judge. On the right of the judge will be found the jury, more or less directly in front of you.

Although it is not usual for witnesses of fact to take notes or documents into the witness box, this is perfectly normal for a forensic scientist or expert witness, who can take a copy of their report into the witness box with them. If anything other than the report needs to be referred to during your evidence-in-chief, your lawyer will need to ask permission for this from the judge. This does make it more straightforward for you because you will not have to juggle a lot of irrelevant papers. Generally speaking, your report should contain details of all the points which are relevant and upon which you might be questioned. Very occasionally you may find yourself being moved away from your area of expertise, in which case say that you are unable to comments on that point. If it is an area on which you are capable of commenting but has not been addressed in your original report, make a mental note of the point so that afterwards you can work backwards and try to find out the reason for your omission.

Once you have been called as a witness to appear in court, possibly sat through hours of other people's evidence and finally asked to give your evidence-in-chief, there is one very important thing to be done. Before any evidence is given by any witness an oath or affirmation must be sworn. There is a fundamental difference between an oath and an affirmation. The oath is one upon which a promise is made to tell the truth. This is sworn on a religious book, which is held in the right hand, and the exact words to be said are read off a card. The oath for the Bible runs along the lines of:

I swear by Almighty God that the evidence I shall give shall be the truth, the whole truth and nothing but the truth.

Other religions have slightly different wording and the religious book will, of course, vary. Although the books of major religions are generally available, religions with a very small congregation are unlikely to have a readily available text upon which to swear an oath. Similarly, an agnostic or atheist would also be unable, or unwilling, to use a religious text for making an oath, but due to historical precedents the swearing of a religious oath is no longer mandatory.

As it is no longer necessary to swear an oath, an affirmation will suffice and is of equal validity to the court. The affirmation runs along these lines:

I do solemnly, sincerely and truly declare and affirm that the evidence I shall give shall be the truth, the whole truth and nothing but the truth.

The start of the affirmation

Although the difference between an affirmation and an oath is now taken as obvious, this was not always so and realistically is still a bit fuzzy around the edges when it comes to sworn oaths of public officials to carry out their duty in a truthful and correct manner. If an oath or affirmation is in writing then the document becomes an affidavit, usually witnessed by a trusted officer of the social group. All of these depend on an assumption of honesty on the part of the person making the sworn statement, which is where the philosophical paradox and foible of the system arises.

(*continued*)

Until the thirteenth century disputed serious crimes could be settled by swearing an oath of denial, by battle (a sort of 'might is right' contest) or by ordeal. Prior to 1215 the Church could be involved in disputed oaths of fact: the disputed case of one person's sworn denial in a serious crime, perhaps with a dead body as evidence. This might be by fire or water with the role of the priest to conjure elements such as fire or water to determine the truth of an oath. The pressure to swear the truth was compounded by the literal belief in the Bible which would therefore result in eternal damnation if you were telling a lie. After 1215 the Roman Church ended the complicity of the Church in England in this process and changed the question from 'guilty or not guilty?' more towards the circumstances surrounding the guilty act.

It is sometimes imagined that the affirmation is a new innovation, but it does have an ancient root. In 1695, during the reign of William III, an Act of Parliament was passed which read:

> An act that the Solemne [sic] Affirmation and Declaration of the people called Quakers shall be accepted instead of an oath in the usual forme [sic].

The Quakers, also known as the Society of Friends, would not take an oath because they believed that one must speak the truth at all times, so swearing to this by Almighty God would imply that this is not the case. It was only in 1978 that the affirmation became codified for anyone who did not want to swear an oath, or would find it difficult. The legislation contains the following paragraph:

> ... above shall apply in relation to a person to whom it is not reasonably practicable without inconvenience or delay to administer an oath in the manner appropriate to his religious belief as it applies in relation to a person objecting to be sworn.

There are many such religions, little known in the West, but of equal importance as any mainstream religion and with their own holy book, which might just not be available to the court.

The paradox alluded to above in all this is a simple one, clearly manifest in the refusal of the Society of Friends mandate. If you tell the truth as part of your daily life then swearing that you will tell the truth is irrelevant. If you do not routinely tell the truth then swearing that you will do so is also irrelevant because swearing that you will tell the truth may be the first lie of your testimony.

The tautology and redundant usage in the oath and affirmation can only be assumed to exist to underline the importance of the words, almost harping back to the medieval process of underlining the torments and damnation that the next life holds for transgressors (see previous box). Whichever method you choose, taking the oath, or affirmation, is best done slowly. Make sure it is clear what you are saying and try not to shuffle your feet while you are reading it; the message that shuffling and mumbling while making an affirmation gives off is not a good one. You should also face in the direction of the judge while reading the card, but if this is a jury trial make sure it is loud enough to be clearly heard by the jury.

Once the oath has been completed your examination-in-chief will begin. This starts off in one of two ways and it is well to ask the barrister beforehand which route they are going to take. The barrister can ask you to give your name and professional address, or the alternative way is for these to be read out so that you can confirm them. Following this you will be asked if the report which the barrister holds up is yours. All those present who need to see the report, including the judge, will have a copy. Next comes a description of your qualifications and expertise relevant to the case being heard. Since most people start a forensic career with a degree, begin there, then go on to your experience which is also relevant to the case being heard. If you are working for the Forensic Science Service you would not expect to appear in court for some considerable time after joining the service, so if it is your first outing as a scientist in court, confine yourself to how many years you have been working as a forensic scientist. If you have published any articles in journals, now is the time to mention them, as long as they are relevant. Some authorities suggest enclosing a more detailed CV in the back of your report, but this is generally unnecessary.

During this examination stay within your field. Although the initial examination will be by the barrister for your side, do not say anything which can be picked up on later by the other side. Perfectly accurate and precise forensic statements can be clouded by being led to make comments outside your area of expertise. If the questions do try to lead you away from the exact area of your report, but still in an area in which you have in-depth knowledge, you can direct a comment to the judge that while able to answer the question in broad terms you were not asked to address this point in your analysis of the evidence. Even if it is only just outside your area or the data covered in your report, if you venture over the line it will be picked up during cross-examination, which will potentially undermine your credibility. There is also another reason why you should always stay within your area of expertise: simply put, you are not in court to venture an opinion on a subject in which you are not an expert. During this examination-in-chief you will be more or less walked through your report to bring out the important points. In criminal cases this can take some time as the issues might be highly technical and require some background explanation for the benefit of both the judge and jury. This is generally true in criminal cases, but in civil cases it may often be a simple case of the judge asking you if you still agree with the findings as laid out in your report. Remember that the business of the court is, and should be, taken very seriously, so the judge, along with counsel for both sides, will have read your report and most likely made notes on it. If for any reason you have doubts, or a reason to modify your opinion, this is the last chance you will get to say so, although it must be said that it is now a bit on the late side and an amended report should have been issued.

When you arrive in the witness box it will be apparent that the judge is just about in front of you, slightly to the right, and the lawyers are to your front left. At this point the process becomes interestingly formal. You will be asked questions by the barrister, but your answers should be directed to the leader of the court – the judge. It is sometimes suggested that the witness stands with their feet a shoulder width apart facing the judge. This will allow you to keep your feet still and turn from the hips to face the barrister as they ask the questions and then back to the judge to give your answer. You may find it more comfortable to stand with your feet at 45 degrees between the barrister and judge, a simple piece of pragmatism as turning your body from the waist through 90 degrees between barrister and judge can be quite tiring in itself. Listen carefully to the lawyer asking the question; it is important that you answer the question precisely, nothing else. This is similar to sitting in front of an examination paper: always read the question thoroughly and answer that, not what you want to answer, or think you are being asked. If the answer is one word, that is all you need – do not embellish or obfuscate the answer with unnecessary details or opinions.

Once you have been asked a question make sure you understand it. Sometimes lawyers can struggle to formulate a question in an area which is a long way out of their area of understanding, which is often the case with matters of a scientific nature. It is worth having a brief conversation around the general area in which you are giving evidence with your counsel to see what level of understanding there is. Do not try to educate the barrister or be patronising, just be aware that there may be more for you to do in understanding what a particular question is trying to find out than in actually answering the question. As there may well be a language problem, that is the right words but not necessarily in the right order, do not be reticent in asking the lawyer to repeat the question, or even to say that you do not fully understand the question and could it be amplified, or phrased in a different way? Once you have heard and understood the question, think about your answer. This is really for the benefit of the court because, although the answer might be easy for you, it must be phrased in such a way that an individual untrained in the subject can grasp the important point and not an unimportant one by mistake. Thinking time is easily gained because you should be familiar with the details of your report and the subjects which it covers and therefore should only require the time it takes to turn from the barrister to give your answer to the judge. If the answer that you are about to give is a lengthy one, watch what the judge is doing. It is most likely that the judge will be taking notes, possibly even writing down what you are saying verbatim, so speak slowly. If the judge is taking notes, move through your answer one sentence at a time and watch the judge's hand. It may seem unnaturally slow, but wait for the judge to stop writing before you move on to the next point. You want your testimony to be as complete as possible for the summing up by the judge; if you rush, important points may be lost and whole parts of your evidence potentially ignored.

After your examination-in-chief you can expect to be cross-examined by the barrister for the other side. This is the process of testing your evidence to see if there are any flaws, but also to extract the truth for the benefit of the court. The cross-examining barrister and their forensic scientist will have been making notes throughout your evidence-in-chief to try and find ways in which they can show that your skills are lacking, or that your opinion is inaccurate and not to be taken as valuable. They will also try to gain information which they can then use for their own benefit in the case. Now, remember that you are working in an adversarial system, so cross-examination can be an uncomfortable and hostile situation, especially for the novice. Questions will be critical and, as sometimes happens, if the case is sound and reliable the cross-examining barrister may get a little more personal than you would like and not just regarding your credibility as a scientist. One way in which the barrister may attempt to get you on the defensive is by mispronouncing your name. This sort of thing has happened to me in court, the effect on me being to raise a smile and almost a laugh. This is because it happens on a regular basis anyway. If it was a deliberate attempt to get me on the back foot it was a mistake by the barrister. Let me explain. As Dr Wilson Wall if I say my name is Wilson, informal, the assumption made is that I am Mr Wilson, easily corrected and so common a mistake that when it happened in court it was amusing to me because I did not feel inclined to correct the barrister, who now had either to correct himself, which he did, or to live with the mistake. If you can just ignore it if the lawyer mispronounces your name, or gets it completely wrong, so much the better as it may be a genuine mistake. If it is deliberate this is all to do with testing you and your evidence to the utmost, which is what the barrister is being paid for. Cross-examination can be a difficult position to be put in, so try to relax and remember that although it may seem personal, it is not. Regard your evidence as something quite separate from you, possibly even produced by another person. The most important thing to do is keep calm. Lawyers will often try to undermine you, your qualifications and your experience, or lack of it, as they see it. There are many ways this can be done and the best lawyers can be extremely subtle. Before looking at some of these ways, note that under no circumstances should you become agitated or angry with the way the cross-examination is going or the lawyer carrying it out. If you do you will slip up – note 'will slip up', not 'may slip up'. Do not try to score points off the lawyer. Although there are a number of reasons for this, two are paramount. The first is that it makes you look petulant and therefore you undermine yourself and your evidence in the eyes of the court. The second is that you are a scientist – you deal with facts, the lawyer deals with words. If you try to have a verbal joust with a lawyer you will almost inevitably lose; they make their living with words and no matter what your personal opinion is about it they are extremely adept at using them. Unhinging you is something that can only help the case for the other side. All sorts of methods can be used to demonstrate that your report is based on unsound principles, or that, even if the principles are sound, the conclusions are flawed. You may feel that you are being prodded into a corner, which is what the lawyer wants. When you are on the defensive you may be tempted to exaggerate your position and the value of your data. Exaggeration is definitely not a good idea, as you may well find yourself presented with a theoretical situation designed to show up the flaw in your position, so besides not losing control, do not alter your position away from that which is in your report. Another interesting and ostensibly innocent way in which your credibility can be undermined is to be asked to explain a technical term or process. Although in normal circumstances you would have no problem answering the question, whatever it is, it can be a little unnerving to have such questions sprung upon you in court. There is another technique which is a favourite among some lawyers and debating societies: namely, the reductionist view, which is usually based on an initial premise which is not incorrect, but is not the whole picture; this is then followed by a leap which in the example I shall give is obviously wrong, but can be just about plausible in the context of a complicated forensic analysis where the flaws in the logic can be glossed over or missed. Tables have four legs; this has four legs, therefore it must be a table. As you can see, there are assumptions, inaccuracies and sleight of hand going on here which we can plainly see, but in a complex analysis it may be more difficult for the jury to spot.

Repetition in the hope of a contradiction, or that you will try to underline a previous answer to the same question by exaggeration, is often tried during cross-examination. Remember what you said previously and what previous questions were as this can save you the problem of tripping over your own past answers. If you are asked the same question twice, possibly in a different way, it is quite reasonable to say 'As I said earlier. . . .' This just emphasises the repetition of the lawyer asking the questions.

Broadly speaking, anything the barrister can do to undermine your analysis of the evidence will be done. Frequently, however, if you have produced a sound report and do not get flustered you will make an excellent impression on the court and come out of the process looking very professional. The way in which you give your evidence is as important as the content itself. Although this may seem odd, since it is facts with which you are, or should be, dealing, it is an unfortunate piece of sociology that juries are at least as influenced by the presentation of evidence as by the evidence itself. This is a very important point; if you are warm and personable towards the court, it will be on your side. The court generally is anyway at the start, but it is easy to alienate the court if you are arrogant or egotistical. Always remember that you are not there to promote yourself, or to be partisan, but there to help the court come to a sensible and correct conclusion on the basis of the evidence, and quite possibly it will be your evidence which is pivotal in the case.

When giving evidence, either evidence-in-chief or cross-examination evidence, you should use short and clear sentences and try to avoid language which is too technical for an average person to understand. To this end it is worth testing out words and phrases on someone who is unfamiliar with the subject. Simplicity is the watchword here – overcomplexity will lose the jury and render your evidence useless. So explain difficult ideas and trains of thought and just because the ideas are as familiar to you as switching on a kettle, they will not be to most of the jury, or the judge. Another aspect of credibility in giving evidence is to avoid slang terms or slang grammar, since they are very easily misunderstood. Be prepared to repeat yourself for the sake of clarity if you think it will help in understanding a difficult point.

It is also worth thinking about your voice, not the accent, but the clarity. It is worth trying to relax your face by using a few facial exercises, preferably in private, but if that is not possible, just smile broadly – you will be surprised how much that will help in clarity of voice. As a long-term method of making sure you can be clearly heard when you are speaking, practise some of the warm-up exercises that singers use. These generally help in annunciation of both vowels and consonants, and can also be useful if you have a stutter, but do remember that singing is generally frowned upon in court.

Although you should defend your position, there is no harm in conceding a valid point or idea. We shall look at sampling techniques in more detail in the chapter covering statistics. Suffice it to say here that you should have a clear understanding of the issues, so when a lawyer suggests that your control, or comparison sample, would be better if it were larger, you can admit that, but then explain why your sample was adequate at the size it was.

There is an unusual aspect to the evidence of a forensic scientist or expert witness: that is, you will be giving evidence of both fact and opinion. The fact may be something as simple as the width of a road, the opinion based on this may be what the road width contributed to a road accident. But do not make assumptions which can be challenged because you have overdone the extrapolation from fact to opinion. It is, without doubt, areas of opinion which will cause most arguments in court. Your evidence of fact should be sound and, unless you have made some errors in your analysis, it should be broadly in agreement with the scientist working with the other side. Consequently you should be very careful about your associated opinion; if you stretch a point, or move out of your area of expertise, you are very likely to be caught out by some clever questioning, helped and directed by the scientist for the other side. It may seem easy to say do not stray from the point, but the questioning lawyer may try and move you in a direction where you are not an expert. Keep a very close eye on what is being asked of you and if it is outside your area, say to the judge that you cannot answer the question for precisely that reason. It will not detract in any way from your evidence.

All this is not to put you off court, or to make you overly defensive when you are giving evidence, it is just to emphasise that it is an adversarial system. Stick to the facts, do not be anything but honest and do not step out of your field of expertise. If for any reason your evidence-in-chief or cross-examination is interrupted, for example a lunch break or an overnight adjournment, you must not discuss the case with anybody, not even your instructing solicitor.

After the cross-examination you will sometimes be re-examined by your own barrister. This is not very common, but if you are it will be to clarify points made during the process of cross-examination. When this is all over you will be told that you can leave the witness box, but unless you are the last expert, or forensic scientist, giving evidence, or you are a witness of fact, you should return to your seat to help your lawyers with their cross-examination of the expert appearing for the other side. This is a very important part of your job. Remember that the lawyer you are dealing with and the lawyer for the other side will most likely not have a technical grasp of the scientific details which you have, even though they may have represented clients in the same sort of case numerous times before. Be prepared to listen in detail to the evidence-in-chief of the scientist from the other side and make notes, so that when your lawyer cross-examines the other scientist you will be prepared to pass notes to the barrister to help direct questions in a coherent manner.

Broadly speaking, appearing in court can be difficult for the novice, but with a few ground rules it will be as stressless as you want it:

1. Go into the court as relaxed as possible.

2. Listen to the question, answer that alone and give yourself time to think.

3. Avoid words and phrases that you would not expect a layman to understand.

4. Stay within your area of expertise – do not be afraid to say that you cannot answer a question for that reason.

5. Do not try to argue with the barrister.

6. Speak clearly and slowly, especially if the judge is making notes.

7. Be brief; if the answer is yes or no, say just that – nothing more.

8. Dress to fit in with your team, avoid the flamboyant – it will distract the jury.

9. You are a professional – enjoy using your skill and knowledge for the benefit of society.

6

Statistics and Statistical Inferences

Part and parcel of the job of a forensic scientist is analysis of data, in whatever form it comes, whether it is the refractive index of a glass sample, the chemical composition of paint or a fingerprint. This may seem self-evident, but analysis is different from collecting data, or from accumulating information. When you have information, data, what do you do with it? This question is important because any court requesting either your report or your presence is going to want an explanation of your results. For this reason alone you should always be clear about what your data does and does not tell you: never over-interpret your data, or claim something for it that is not wholly defendable, because it will be challenged.

Whatever sort of forensic data you have, a fundamental point is to understand the difference between precision and accuracy and how they relate to the two major error types, statistical and systematic.

These relate to each other in a very simple manner: systematic errors affect accuracy, statistical errors affect precision. Accuracy refers to the proximity of results to the theoretical truth and may be scattered around, say, the true mean, so would give a true result. Precision refers to the position of the measured mean to the true mean.

With large statistical and systematic errors there are both low precision and low accuracy. These are very difficult to deal with as there is no clear method of extracting meaningful information from the data as it tends to look random.

Forensic Science in Court: The Role of the Expert Witness   Wilson Wall
© 2009 W. J. Wall

If we think of an archery target in this situation the distribution of arrows would be all over the target. On the other hand, if there are a large statistical error and low systematic error there would be low precision but high accuracy. Using the analogy of the archery target, the arrows would be scattered widely about the centre of the target and although a single measurement is of little value, repeated measurements will ensure that the correct conclusion is drawn. It is obvious from this that repeated measurements can improve the accuracy of a result by moving the measured mean closer to the true mean, but it is also important to realise that eventually there is no point in continually adding measurements to the total because the mean will not significantly alter and residual statistical errors may become more important and spurious conclusions arise.

Referring to Figure 6.1, when small statistical errors but large systematic errors are encountered it can give the spurious impression of accuracy because the results are all very close together, but this is not the case. In this situation there is high precision and low accuracy; with our target the arrows would all be closely grouped together, but to one side of the centre. These sorts of errors are easily dealt with by altering one of the parameters to move the grouping towards the true mean, without compromising the accuracy of the measurements. If this is done, then the ideal situation is achieved with both statistical and systematic errors being small and the results highly reliable.

There is a second aspect to forensic statistics which cannot be overemphasised, indeed it is also a part of our language which is frequently misused – the word unique. Unique is not unique in being misused; another example of misuse is the word sterile. Understanding these words may be of importance in many ways, especially when you are tempted to use them inappropriately in a written report. When something is sterile, that is it. It is devoid of life and it is not possible for one thing to be more sterile than another, it either is or it is not, so there is no such thing as 'partially sterile'. This gives us a clear idea of unique. Now, while ideas of sterility may seem strange in a forensic situation – after all, you are not likely to need sterility in a test – it can be taken as an example of a word with a very specific meaning that is often misused. This brings us to use of the word 'unique'.

Be very careful when using the word 'unique': something is unique, or it is not, it cannot be more unique, or very unique. It has often been said that fingerprints are unique. Actually they are not, but it is probably true to say that at any given time it is extremely unlikely that two people will share the

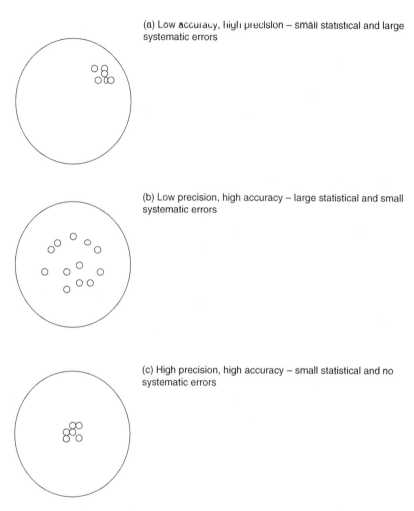

(a) Low accuracy, high precision – small statistical and large systematic errors

(b) Low precision, high accuracy – large statistical and small systematic errors

(c) High precision, high accuracy – small statistical and no systematic errors

Figure 6.1 Precision and accuracy – shooting at a target.

same fingerprints. So uniqueness can be ruled out for two reasons: first, the probability of two people sharing the same fingerprint, although vanishingly small, is still finite; and the second reason is a numerical one based on a simple question – how many different fingerprints are possible? A simple demonstration using numbers can show that the idea of unique fingerprints is incorrect because there are not an infinite number of fingerprints available. If we were to arrange all the atoms in the universe (a very large number, but not an infinite one) there would still be a numerical value to the permutations, admittedly not a calculable one, but not an infinite one either. On the end of a finger of finite dimensions there is a finite number of atoms, so even if we could detect the difference of a single atom there would still be a finite number of different fingerprints possible.

The reason for labouring this point is that barristers make their living using language and inappropriate words may well be picked up on because when statistics come to court they are not necessarily understood, but the words which summarise them are, so be very careful that you understand the words you use in your reports and testimony. In statistical terms fingerprints are in a very odd situation because they have developed a sense of infallibility which is not easily justified. The problem lies in the nature of the evidence – fingerprints are rarely perfect, but often usually smeared, or partial, so the fingerprint analyst has to give an opinion regarding the match between what was found at a crime scene and those taken from an individual under controlled conditions. This raises an interesting conundrum for the court because, without knowing the error rate of incorrect inclusions and exclusions, it is very difficult to determine how reliable a declared result is. Consequently, it is possible for the fingerprint evidence of one expert to be challenged by another. Fingerprints are rarely taken as evidence in isolation, unlike DNA evidence, so it could be argued that a partial fingerprint may well have some probative value for the court. The reason for the perceived high value of fingerprint evidence is simply an historical one. They were one of the earliest methods of identification which actually worked, rather than could be made to work. This was based on the recognition that in most situations an individual's fingerprints could be used as an invariant biological signature. It is true, however, that although it has been declared that there is no error rate with fingerprints, this is a scientific impossibility: the error rate just has not been measured and there are people who have been included as suspects on the basis of incorrectly measured fingerprints.

In other areas of forensic science it is also common not to have a statistical basis for the interpretation of results, but a direct comparison between two or more items, such as bullets or paint samples, and a match declared or not as the case may be. These can be compared with reference samples, as in the case of dyes or paints, or between a crime scene sample and a sample from a suspect item, such as bullets when a discarded gun is found. This may be thought of as a simple correlation, relating two variables to each other. This is slightly different to the process of making a predictive correlation, which in its simplest form is usually done from data which can be analysed graphically in two dimensions, such as height and weight. Now in this case it would be reasonable to expect that taller people are heavier than short ones, but once you start thinking about overweight individuals, the picture, the correlation, becomes more difficult to interpret. In statistical analysis, where everyone is an individual, absolute correlations are generally hard to find. Correlations, designated r, of 1, that is perfect association, such as if you buy 1 kg of apples you will pay £X and if you buy 2 kg of apples you will pay £$2X$, are very rare. You are more likely to find a correlation of less than 1.

Correlation coefficients range from -1 to $+1$ (see Figure 6.2). This range indicates that when there is a correlation between two events, such as when the price of an item goes up, you buy less, this is a negative correlation. Conversely, when certain items go up in price, there might be panic buying which results in a positive correlation between price and sales. Needless to say, when the correlation coefficient is 0 there is no relationship between the two measured variables. So what does the correlation coefficient tell us? Simply this: if a correlation is 0 between two variables then we learn nothing from one variable that allows us to predict what the other variable will be. If the correlation is 1, either positive or negative, we have all the information to predict from one variable what the other variable will be. That should be fairly straightforward – it is the bits in between where confusion arises. The point is that 1 is a peculiar number, for example $1 \times 1 = 1$ and $1/1 = 1$. When it comes to the numbers in between, interpretation has to be guided by the way in which correlation coefficients are calculated, so with extreme values of correlations it is intuitive and when it comes to intermediate values it is not. A correlation of 0.5 does not tell us that we have half the information from one variable to predict the other, but 0.7071 does. You can work this out because the correlation coefficient operates in two dimensions and like many statistical calculations involves a 'square' so that there is no negative value to be worked on.

Intimately associated with the correlation coefficient is linear regression. There are other forms of regression which can be calculated, but these are not generally used in forensic analyses. Linear regression no longer carries the original biological implication that it started with, but the phrase is used as shorthand for predicting one variable from another. In 1885 Francis Galton

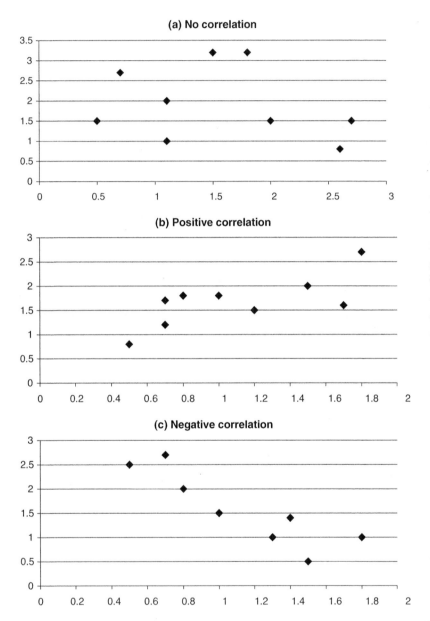

Figure 6.2 (a) No correlation between the two variables. (b) Positive correlation between values: as X goes up, Y tends to go up as well. (c) Negative correlation between two values: as X goes up so Y goes down.

wrote a paper with the title 'Regression towards mediocrity in hereditary stature' in which he observed that offspring of tall parents tended to be shorter than their parents and offspring of short parents tended to be taller than their parents. He referred to this as regression towards a biological norm. Regression is the way in which one variable can be predicted from another. This is done by constructing regression lines: that is, for any set of data which can be plotted on an X and Y axis there are two possible regression lines, X on Y and Y on X. These two lines usually differ from each other as they are each constructed from a different premise but using the same technique. The lines are produced by the method of least squares. The line Y on X is used to predict Y from X. It is drawn by locating a line in a position such that the sum of the squares of the distance from the data points to the line parallel to the Y axis is at a minimum. To produce the line X on Y, predicting X from Y, a line is drawn which minimises the sum of squares of distances from the data points to the line when the distances are measured parallel to the X axis. This is shown in Figure 6.3.

The two regression lines are separate except when the correlation coefficient is either $+1$ or -1, that is an exact correlation between two variables, such that knowing one variable means it is possible to know the other variable with absolute certainty and without any other knowledge. In this, rare,

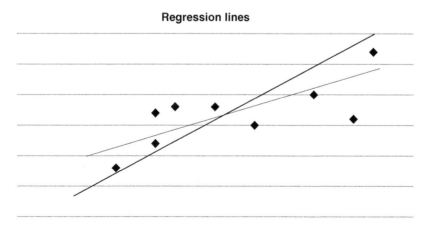

Regression lines

Figure 6.3   From scattered points two regression lines can be drawn, except when all the points fall on a single line, in the case of a correlation coefficient of $+1$ or -1.

circumstance, there will be a single regression line. As the degree of variability increases, as shown by a deviation of the correlation coefficient away from unity, so the angle between the two regression lines at their crossover point will increase. In the extreme case of no relationship between the two measurements, when the correlation coefficient is 0, the two regression lines will be at right angles to each other.

Sir Francis Galton

Francis Galton has had a significant influence upon forensic science, but it is not just in this arena of science that he was active. Born in the UK near Birmingham in 1822, he was a cousin of Charles Darwin. He was educated in Birmingham and London where he attended King's College, and then graduated from Trinity College Cambridge in medicine. He travelled extensively after graduation in both North and South Africa, publishing *Narrative of an Explorer in Tropical South Africa* (1853) and *Art of Travel* (1855). He was interested in descriptive meteorology, which led to the publication of the first weather map in *The Times* in 1875. His publication *Meteorographia* (1863) laid the foundation for modern weather maps, with many of his symbols still being used. After these studies Galton moved more and more towards the study of heredity, which was in its infancy with no clear laws of inheritance having been laid down, which would come later with Gregor Mendel. This involved Galton in looking at such conditions as colour blindness and fingerprints, a subject upon which he wrote his book *Finger Prints* (1892). All of these studies required a detailed knowledge of another nascent subject, statistics. It was here that he coined the word regression. Although statistical analysis is now a common activity throughout scientific endeavour, the start of the subject and most of its early development lays with biology and, more specifically, genetics.

One area where a database and stringent statistical analysis are essential is where there is a probability of coincidental matches being found. Although this should really extend across most, if not all, forensic investigations, it rarely does. A rigorous statistical approach has been adopted for what has become the most important method of personal identification – DNA analysis. This particular type of analysis serves as the gold standard in forensic analysis, because it has taken new technology and demonstrated that it is robust and reliable by analysing samples with tried and tested statistical methods which are themselves mathematically proven methods. Unfortunately, although the statistical techniques are sound, sometimes the interpretation of what they tell us is not. This is generally because of a misunderstanding of the way in which statistics are expressed in words.

An example of the misrepresentation of statistics can be found in the phrase 'the exception which proves the rule'. At first glance this does not make a great deal of sense, since an exception cannot prove anything in the modern sense, but consider the exact meaning of proof – testing. This then becomes 'the exception which tests the rule', which now makes sense. If you have the luck to travel from London to Birmingham in the UK you will pass towards the centre of Birmingham where, at rooftop level, there is a building with a very ornately coloured and embossed coat of arms at the top. This is emblazoned with the words 'Gun Barrel Proof House'. This refers not to the building being strong against gun barrels, but to the fact that it was here that gun barrels were tested, or proved, for strength. This was done in a measured, but originally unsystematic way. Simply put, the barrel was sealed, spiked and a charge set off in the breach. If the barrel exploded then it was not strong enough and that batch of arms was failed. It was the exception which proved, tested, the rule.

So, back to the statistical misrepresentations which you will come across because of the way they are expressed in words, rather than mathematical notation. The most important one is the 95% certainty, usually reported as the 95% confidence interval. This should be explained by reference to what it is that you are testing. This is simply expressed as the null hypothesis, which is a falsifiable hypothesis. An example of this would be 'there are no fairies at the bottom of my garden'. This can be falsified by finding a fairy at the bottom of the garden, but the alternative 'there are fairies at the bottom of my garden' cannot be falsified because not finding fairies may simply be interpreted as not having looked hard enough. So we set up a null hypothesis to see if we can reject it by statistical analysis. This can sometimes be tricky, and sometimes we do not realise what it is that we are testing.

Setting up a null hypothesis to be tested and then carrying out a probability calculation can give an erroneous impression of certainty and this can be referred back to our notion of both accuracy and precision. If we were to say that a 95% confidence interval for the parameter which we are testing ranges from, say, -1 to $+1$, then it would seem that our parameter is between these two values with 95% confidence, but this is not what this statistic tells us at all. What it actually tells us is that if we repeat the same experiment then we will find that the unknown value will be somewhere in the confidence interval for 95% of the time. This is actually quite different to saying we are 95% certain that our value is correct.

If we return to the concept of precision and accuracy, it becomes immediately apparent that using statistical analysis may well help in increasing the precision, but it may still be that the results are inaccurate because of systematic errors resulting in our confidence interval being set up in the wrong place. Always treat this sort of analysis, when reading it and when carrying it out, with caution. This is all associated with probability and odds and is the most frequently seen statistical analysis in forensic science. Unfortunately, odds have the association with betting on a future event, trying to see into the future, which is not generally what forensics is about. This strange process can be demonstrated by a simple example. Using a standard pack of cards, what is the probability of randomly picking the ace of diamonds without looking? It should be 1 in 52, and it is. Now, turn this around and the odds are different when you are not predicting the future. If you pick a card at random and it is the ace of spades, what is the probability of that? It is not 1in 52 because you were not predicting that card, the probability is 1 in 1, or simply 1, remembering that probabilities run from 0 (never) to 1(certain). This can also be applied to such things as winning a lottery. You choose your numbers and they have a probability of, say, 1 in 40 million of coming up, but if you win the probability that your numbers came up would be 1, because they did. This is the difference between the probability of an event happening and the probability that an event happened, with no reference to the past. So probabilities have different values depending on whether they are predictive or descriptive of an event which has already taken place and even then it is possible with a mangled form of logic to go back before the event occurred and give odds on that event taking place when you already know the outcome.

An example of probability – a trick with three cards

Probability can be an elusive thing to understand; it can be manipulated by the unscrupulous and misunderstood by the unsophisticated. This demonstration ideally requires two people, one as dealer/manipulator and one as player. All you need are three playing cards, or three of anything which are different and can be laid flat so that the difference cannot be seen, such as three coins of the same denomination but different dates. We will stick to the cards here. One of the cards should be clearly distinguished from the other two, say an ace.

Right, the dealer lays the three cards face down, knowing which one is the ace. The player now has to guess which of the three cards is the ace without looking. That one is moved, but neither dealer nor player can look at it. The probability of the player picking the ace is, of course, 1 in 3.

The dealer, who knows which of the remaining two cards is the ace, turns over a card which he therefore knows to be an ordinary card. Since the original choice of a card had a probability of 1 in 3 the remaining cards have a probability of being the ace of 2 in 3. Since we now have one card chosen and one card turned over to reveal that it is not the ace, there are two cards still face down. What is the probability of the card originally chosen being the ace? The natural, though incorrect, assumption is to say that since there are two cards it should be 50:50. If it had started with only two cards then it would be 50:50, but there were three cards, so the card which the player originally chose had a probability of 1/3 of being the ace, while the other two had a probability of 2/3.

Although the dealer has now revealed one of the two remaining cards as not being the ace, the two cards which are still face down do not change their probability of being the ace: the probability for the player's card is 1/3 and for the dealer's 2/3, that is the probability is fixed. So if the dealer asks the player 'do you want to exchange your card with the one I have?', the player should always make the exchange.

If you try this yourself you will find that, as the player, overall you will win 2/3 of the time.

The clearer use of probability in forensic science is most often based on relative frequencies, that is making repeated measurements to create a database from which the frequency of occurrence of a paint type, or a DNA profile, or a tyre tread can be calculated. It is a simple construction: making repeated measurements (N) and finding that a specific value appears r times allows for the calculation of the relative frequency as r/N. The value of this sort of analysis is that it can give an idea of just how likely it is for that particular sample or profile to turn up by chance. Ideally, however, we would like to be able to interpret the statistics so that we could get a much more intuitive answer than classical statistics will give us. Not surprisingly, frustration with statistics has resulted in a different form being used which does precisely that and is ideal for use in forensic applications, while making the resultant analysis clear and easy to understand for use in court, which, after all, is where all the evidence and statistical analysis will end up.

This new statistical approach was first worked out by a Presbyterian minister by the name of Thomas Bayes, hence we still refer to it as Bayesian statistics, even though it has been widely developed since first described in the eighteenth century. Thomas Bayes (1702–1761) was quite prolific in his own lifetime, although mostly not published under his own name. Precisely why he developed such an interest in statistics is unknown, but forensic scientists the world over are glad that he did. His major work was published in 1763 by his friend Richard Price, but under the name of Bayes. I will not go into the mathematical structure of Bayesian statistics, but I will describe some of the salient points about it.

What Bayes effectively managed to do was turn the classical ideas of statistics on their head. At the time this was clearly seen as a breakthrough in thinking, but unfortunately it gradually fell out of favour as it was seen by later generations of statisticians to be too experimenter centred, just too subjective to be reliable. Closer examination, however, shows us that this is not so and in fact it can render far better the insights which we want from a statistical analysis than conventional methods can. Part of the reason for the attitude of later statistical experimenters was that Bayesian statistics involved the experimenter's beliefs. Simply put, instead of applying a fixed population number to be sampled it was possible to say that the experimenter could decide when there were enough measurements, however large or small this value was. At the same time, finding a probability from this and then multiplying it by your prior beliefs, or prior odds, results in a value which is exactly what is required – the probability of an event occurring with 95% certainty. This is important in forensic science when taken to court because, unless the data is presented in the correct form, the jury will make the naive, and incorrect, assumption that a 95% probability of a match between two samples, from a database and a crime scene, equates to a 95% probability of guilt.

This leads on to databases and their construction. Databases come in two broad forms, frequency databases and databases of named individuals. These are quite separate databases and serve quite separate functions. The most common database form and the one most well known is the DNA database. It is here that the two broad categories are most easily demonstrated and also the myriad different ways in which databases can be used and abused. Of the two database types it is the anonymous database which is the easiest to understand; it is also the database which has the least contentious issues surrounding it. The primary thing to remember about DNA profile databases is that they are not complete sequences, they are a collection of numbers representing the number of repeats at a set of specific loci. These loci are specifically chosen for their high variation between individuals and their inability to be found among standard food materials, commensal species, such as rats, and domestic animals. This makes a DNA database about as complicated as databases which deal with such things as the chemical composition of explosives, or paint. The purpose of an anonymous database is to allow us to determine exactly how often we would expect to find that profile, or chemical composition of paint. Now, although tastes in car colour change and are different from country to country, tastes in DNA tend not to. By that I mean that we tend to have a balanced collection of DNA repeats which do not vary very much from generation to generation – the Hardy–Weinberg equilibrium. There is, of course, a measurable mutation rate, which is one reason that care has to be exercised when using these profiles for paternity disputes, but other than that, because the overall database is made up of several generations over a period of time and relationships between the various individuals are mostly quite tenuous, the population database which gives us our repeat frequency within the population is a reliable reflection of the true state of affairs.

Asking the right questions

Asking the wrong question when assessing the probability of an event, such as leaving a mark, can have profound affects on the result. In general terms the only correct question runs along the lines of 'How much does the evidence change the probability that the accused left the evidence at the scene?' If this question is asked, the size of the database generating the probability within a population is usually not important once a reasonable size is achieved – with increasing numbers the frequency of a characteristic will not alter. This is particularly important when looking at highly variable biological markers such as DNA, but also other tests. An example of this can be found in the case of the Birmingham Six, detailed elsewhere.

So, the anonymous database tells us the frequency with which we can expect to find an allele, or a paint type, or a specific chemical composition of an explosive. It therefore gives us a calculable probability that if we find a match between two materials, whether it be DNA or a chemical analysis that originated from the same person, in the case of DNA, or the same factory in the case of a chemical analysis.

The difference, though, is that DNA is directly relatable to an individual, whereas chemical analysis can only be related directly to the manufacturing company. So we might find out who made a particular product and the frequency with which it is found in the general population and this would give us an idea of the probability that an event is associated with the owner of a product, whether a car or other manufactured item. What such a database will not contribute to the probity of a case is an exact statement of exclusion of an individual; if guilt is implied by association with a chemical analysis, exoneration by there not being a chemical match is unhelpful. This is exactly what DNA evidence can do. With a DNA profile, if there is a match between two profiles we can calculate the probability that they originated from the same individual, remembering that this is never a certainty, but when we have an exclusion the situation is different. If a DNA profile from a crime scene is different to that from an accused individual, we can say with absolute certainty that the individual did not supply the DNA.

With the change in the way in which evidence is sorted and held, the old adage that DNA evidence is best when used to exonerate no longer holds true because, while in cases of rape a difference between the DNA profile of the sperm and that of the accused is proof that the sperm in the rape case did not come from the accused, the situation can become more complicated in robberies. When a cigarette end is picked up at a crime scene and DNA profiles produced, the obvious assumption is that the same standards apply – they do not. This is because, while it may be easy to demonstrate the originator of the sample, it may be impossible to show exactly where and when a sample was contaminated with the DNA of the accused. With a vaginal swab the DNA obviously came from the assailant, but a planted cigarette end? Care with all things, logic and common sense are very important before you put a signature to your report.

With databases of named individuals, this is exactly what they are: DNA profiles of named individuals; when stopped, arrested or even just cautioned and a mouth swab is taken, your DNA profile is taken and put on a named DNA database. This allows for data trawling when trying to match a crime sample to a named database.

The way in which this works is quite simple in principle, but, interestingly, complicated in the way it is carried out. When a sample is taken from an individual and a profile produced, the process can go in one of two ways, depending upon the jurisdiction. Either it can move to finding out the frequency of that profile within the community and then see if there are matching profiles on the DNA database of profiles from crime scenes, or it can work in the opposite direction. This means that a sample taken from an arrested individual is profiled, checked to see if there are any matching profiles from a scene of crime and then a calculation of a match being found by chance made, using the DNA profile frequency database. This second method of calculating an association is probably preferable if only because it is the more transparent and easily understood method of coming to a conclusion. Whichever way the calculation is made, the result should be the same.

When using databases it should be remembered that there is going to be a measure of uncertainty associated with any trawl of data. The level of inappropriate associations will vary depending on the type of comparison being made, some things being intrinsically less variable than others. In this respect DNA evidence is one of the most unlikely to have a false attribution to an individual, but other databases are not so discriminating. With these sorts of databases used for comparison a simple argument can be made that the more comparisons which are attempted, the more likely it becomes that a false association is found. Now, while with effectively digital information, such as DNA, this is a very unlikely situation, with fingerprints, where interpretation is primarily subjective, finding a match will tend to adhere to this model. It is akin to the idea that if you are looking for the North American 'Bigfoot' and believe it to exist, if you look hard enough you will eventually find it – even if in reality it does not exist. Such is the risk with databases that are not rigorously controlled. So what this tells us is that as databases grow larger, the chance that we will find a match also becomes larger.

With characteristics which are relatively common within a population, the chance finding becomes a significant event. For example, a paint sample from a 'hit and run' car accident has a frequency of use of, say, 1 in 10 vehicles, so if we trawled a database of paint types from known vehicles, we could expect to find a match 10% of the time. Put numerically, on this basis if we consulted a database of 1000 known vehicles we would expect to find 100 matches. This does not reduce the evidential value of the finding; the important question is the probability of finding the match if the person under suspicion was not responsible for the crime. Consequently, if we know the frequency, in this example 1 in 10, the size of the database does not matter because we would always expect a match rate of 10%, and if we know the total number of vehicles on the road we could work out the exact number of vehicles we would expect to have matching paint.

The situation is a little more complicated when we start off without the population frequency of a characteristic. In this situation we have no idea how many matches we would expect to find by chance alone, so if we find one match we represent the probability as 1/the number of entries in the database. This should be self-evident, similarly, for a database of x entries, and however many matches that are found (n) the numerical probability is n/x, so the evidential value is dependent upon the size of the database. If you think of extremes, a database with 10 entries and one match will produce 1/10, but with one match in a database of 1 million the evidence of a match is much more powerful.

As with all databases the constituent members must represent the population from which they come. This is as true for databases of people as for car paints. If only one paint manufacturer submits data or samples for testing, the database against which samples can be compared is going to skewed, almost to the point of uselessness. While a database of biometric data may seem to have the same restrictions, happily humanity is far more uniform on the large scale than people seem to realise. So with no bias being deliberately introduced into database construction, fingerprints and DNA databases become a fair representation of the population at large. If there was pressing evidence that criminals were genetically different from the general population, then we could rightly say that the database was skewed, since criminals are overrepresented in these databases. Since there is no substantive evidence for this we can conclude that this is not so.

An interesting aspect of DNA databases is that with the large numbers of different genetic loci which are looked at using STR analysis (Short Tandem Repeat analysis), the concept of racial differences has broken down. Some DNA profiles, usually the rare ones, are marginally more common in some ethnic groups, so when a calculation as to the probability of finding a match by chance is made, it is made across different ethnic groups. What is presented to the court is the least likely finding, the one which is most in favour of the defendant, even if they were not ostensibly from that ethnic group. This will make little difference to the presented probability, as presented to the court, because the figures only vary numerically and very rarely, if ever, by an order of magnitude. The numbers representing the probability of a match being found by chance are so great that they are essentially incomprehensible.

When DNA profiling was first used in court, probabilities in some courts in the USA were quoted for the chance of a match being found that were greater than 1 in the population of the world. This was based not on finding a match, but on calculating the accumulated probability of a particular DNA profile. This opened up an interesting line of argument for the defence which was erroneous and misleading, but potentially very effective.

The argument ran thus – if the probability of my client having the same profile as the DNA profile from the crime scene is so incredibly unlikely, greater than the population of the planet, then surely my client could not possibly have such a profile and therefore the DNA evidence is flawed. This remarkable and incorrect line of reasoning was tried in an apparent effort to confuse the jury, but once the judiciary had a hold on the slowly developing area of statistics in court, this stopped.

Although this is a good example that the expression of statistics in court is potentially very tricky, you have to be able to express a probability without confusing the jury. It has long been understood that for most people the concept of large numbers is extremely difficult; this simply reflects the human scale of most of what we do. So we all know what 100 is as a concept: a hundred years is a great age for a human, a hundred things may or may not be a lot, that is our perception in the context of 100. Thinking about 1000 years is a bit more difficult to conceptualise, maybe we can imagine a thousand 'things', but as the numbers get larger and the concepts more abstract, the problems arise. This can be daunting: it takes understanding and imagination to perceive, for example, the age of the planet, around 4.5 thousand million years, since our Western calendar dates back only 2000 years; it is no wonder that religious leaders balk at the theory of evolution – they may be incapable of perceiving the concept of a million years, let alone a thousand million years and then four and a half times that number. Do a simple calculation to see how many 2000-year-old civilisations could be fitted into that span of time.

The same problem crops up in court when purely numerical data is presented, the numbers being simply too large to manage. But there is a solution. By using a Bayesian statistical approach we can simplify the method of expression to a point where the jury will hear something that they understand, without being bombarded by numbers. This takes the approach where the forensic scientist, you, is trusted, your results are not partisan and you are disinterested in the outcome of the court case, and you can be relied upon to give objective evidence concerning your area of expertise. Simple – use words. So when a forensic scientist takes, for example, DNA evidence into court, the scale of explanations will be from a weak link between the accused and the crime scene through to extremely strong support for the hypothesis that the accused is the originator of the crime sample. This is a verbal interpretation of a numerical calculation:

- If the probability is from 1 to 10, this is described as a weak link.

- If the probability is from 10 to 100, this lends moderate support.

- If the probability is from 100 to 1000, this is moderately strong support.

- If the probability is from 1000 to 10,000, this is strong support.

- If the probability is from 10,000 to 1 million, this is very strong support.

- If the probability is from 1 million onwards, this is extremely strong support.

All to the hypothesis that the accused is the originator of a crime scene sample.

Now, generally the probabilities which are presented in court for DNA evidence are well over 1 million, indeed so far over 1 million that the numbers are huge. If the court wants to see the figures that is quite in order, but generally the defence lawyer will already have seen the results of the forensic analysis and had them explained and clarified. Generally speaking the numbers, the probability of a random match, will not be presented in court unless the value is significant, either very small or very large. There can be problems with this sort of expression of odds in words when the defendant claims it was his brother who did it. Most violent crimes are perpetrated by men, so I excuse myself from appearing sexist on this account.

If the brother was responsible, and there is a match between his and not his brother's DNA, which we might not have access to, we need to have some method of finding out the probability of two brothers having the same DNA profile. There is a point here in that if there is no reason to suspect the brother it is unreasonable to ask for a sample – samples are stored, so a refusal is quite normal; nobody wants their genetic data on record unless it is legally required and even then they probably do not.

So, if an individual claims that it was a sibling, how can we resolve the situation? Well, we can simply make a calculation based on Mendelian inheritance. This is an aspect of genetics with which you should be not just be familiar with, but comfortable in carrying out the calculations associated with it. Briefly, the calculation which we can do to ascertain the probability of two individuals sharing the same DNA profile depends on few variables, the two most important ones being the number of points of comparison which are used and the degree of relatedness of the two individuals. Currently DNA profiles are constructed from STR data. STRs are simple repeats which vary in number between individuals; the profile is constructed by counting the number of repeats. Since there are two alleles for each STR, which can be either homozygous (the same) or heterozygous (different), there are two values for each STR. Taking the case of a single STR and two parents, both heterozygous and both different from each other, there are four possible outcomes. If we introduce another STR there are eight and with three STRs there are 64 possible combinations. In practice the number of STR systems in use exceeds 10, so the maximum probability of two siblings sharing the same profile is in excess of 1 million to 1 against. This is the extreme value because it is very unusual for an individual to be heterozygous at every measured STR and for both parents not to share at least some of the STR values, so in general terms the probability is less than this, being somewhere between that value and the other extreme. The other extreme would be where both parents are homozygous at every STR and identical to each other, in which case the probability of siblings having the same profile would be 1, that is they would have to be the same because the parents have no STRs to re-sort at meiosis to form new combinations of alleles. The true probability lies between these two extremes and it is possible to produce a robust statistical demonstration of the most likely probability, but this is generally not required.

As individuals become genetically more distant from each other, such as cousins, so the probability of their sharing a profile becomes less and less likely. These are calculations which do not require access to a database; they are calculated from simple and fundamental principles of genetics. At the same time, having access to a very large database with data on large numbers of people, in fact it must be a significant sample of the population, enables a data-trawling exercise to be carried out which can be astonishingly productive for the pursuit of justice, although there must be robust safeguards when using this technique, as we shall discuss in the next chapter.

Given a large enough database and a powerful enough computer, all of the combinations and permutations which we discussed above regarding relatives, both close, as in the case of a sibling or parent, or more distant as in the case of uncles and aunts, can be compared to find whether an unknown suspect is related to them. This process of data trawling, that is sifting through all possibilities, does have limitations because under these circumstances we are dealing with a probability, not a certainty, and the probability will not lie in the 'unlikely to be by chance' end of the probability curve.

Just such a situation has occurred. With the enormous size of the UK DNA database, it has become possible to associate family members with a crime, even though the DNA of the perpetrator was not available for comparison. This was the first time in the world that such a technique was used to apprehend a felon. It was fortuitous that data was available from the DNA database and the final results were impressive. This particular story of data trawling was possible only because the database of named individuals was so large that it was worth trying to see whether DNA from an unknown person could be associated with any of those who were on the database of named individuals, who were a relative of the unknown person. The process is one of immense complexity involving huge amounts of computing power to look for people who may be related to the unknown blood sample.

The story starts when a brick is dropped from a bridge over the M3 motorway in Surrey, UK, in March 2003 and goes through the windscreen of a lorry, hitting the driver in the chest and causing fatal injuries. The driver, Michael Little, who was 53, managed to steer the lorry onto the hard shoulder and bring it to a stop before he succumbed to his injuries. He was discovered by a passing police patrol car when one of the officers noticed his body lying across the steering wheel, more than three hours after the event. The questions asked at this stage were simple to frame but not always easy to answer. They ranged from 'how did a brick come to hit the windscreen of Mr Little's lorry?' to 'who threw it?'. Many of these questions were easy to answer: the brick came from the footbridge over the motorway, it could not have fallen from a vehicle, therefore it must have been dropped or thrown by an individual.

Of interest to the police was the blood on the brick which DNA profiling demonstrated did not come from Michael Little, so the reasonable suggestion was that it came from the assailant. Quite how it came to be on the brick would remain a mystery for some time. Once profiled it was apparent that the DNA on the brick not only did not come from Little, but also was not from any individual on the DNA database. At this time the UK DNA database contained 2.35 million entries, so it was thought that it would be potentially useful to trawl what was available just to see if any family matches came up. It turned out that there was a possible relative who had been profiled for an unrelated reason, and this putative relative came from the same area of England, in Surrey, in fact the same town. So the question was whether samples could be obtained from male relatives of the person whose DNA profile they had. It was going to have to be male relatives because determination of sex from a DNA sample is quick and easy and it had been shown to be male.

It was also easy and straightforward to associate one Craig Harman with the DNA on the brick once a sample of DNA was taken from him. Harman worked in a sports shop and was living with his girlfriend in a town by the name of Frimley. On the night in question he had been out drinking with friends in a nearby town, Camberley, and by his own account had drunk a considerable amount. On the way home Harman tried breaking into a car and it was at this point that he cut his hand. Further on he and his friend picked up two bricks from a garden and then dropped, or threw, them onto the motorway. One car swerved to avoid the obstacle, but Little had no such luck and the brick went through the windscreen in front of him. For this act Harman was given a six-year sentence for manslaughter. When picked up and profiled originally he denied all connections with the incident; it was only when confronted with the evidence that he admitted to the crime. At the time of the incident Harman was 19 years old and had an apparent lack of knowledge of physics. Dropping a brick from a bridge is not just a case of the velocity of the projectile when it hits the ground, or the vehicle, indeed that is a relatively small part of the problem. In the UK at the time of the incident the speed limit on motorways was 70 miles per hour, roughly speaking 120 km/h, so the stored energy in the brick was equivalent to the brick being thrown at the lorry at 120 km/h. It is unlikely that anyone on the planet could hurl something the size of a brick at that speed without a mechanical aid, so dropping a brick from a bridge is as bad as throwing it. This case demonstrated the immense value of DNA and, with the correct software, DNA trawling. It is quite possible that this was a lucky association, but with the increasing number of STR sites which are looked at this is unlikely. The converse is also true: if an exclusion is found this is absolute.

It is always necessary, with any data set, to be aware that for an inclusion, paint, fingerprints or DNA, a probability is arrived at where the match is not by chance. With an exclusion this is not the case at all. If you find an exclusion, that is the fingerprints do not match, or the DNA profile is different, then the exclusion is absolute. It is not possible to make an association because there is no probability associated with it. The simplest example would be a car accident which left red paint and part of the vehicle, painted in red by the manufacturer, at the scene; there is no point in looking for a blue car because no blue car was involved in the accident. Without doubt the most powerful aspect of forensic science is that it can completely exonerate an individual, based on the simple adage 'no match – no association'.

The statistical association between a crime sample and an individual is not always easy to interpret. As we have noted previously, it is necessary to give some measure of probability when declaring a match, not just to the likelihood of the match being real, but in some circumstances to the probability that the match is false, a false positive. In diagnostic situations there is a routine for stating the error rate, which is rarely, if ever, done in forensic circles. This is not a criticism, or a suggestion that the analysis was carried out incorrectly, or samples mixed, but simply that with complicated analytical work things go wrong for a variety of reasons. Diagnostics and forensics have a lot in common in this respect, though the approach is quite different. In diagnostics it is seen as normal to make a statement regarding the reliability of the test being carried out. In forensic applications it is not. This is unfortunate as it lends an air of infallibility to a subject under increasing scrutiny.

Consider a different test, say a pregnancy test, and let us give (fictional) odds of its being positive when there is no pregnancy of, say, 1 in 100. With no false negatives, that is the pregnancy test will not indicate there is no pregnancy where there is one, it is the false positive results that are important. So for every 100 tests we could expect 1 false positive. The test has not given an acceptably true result, consequently if you tested 100 individuals who had not had sex, you would still expect 1 false result. Discounting the distress to the individual, the statistical analysis may make us wonder about the validity of the test. If you add to this the possibility of false negatives, the situation becomes even more complicated.

While some processes are intrinsically impossible to quantify statistically, such as handwriting or fingerprints, and so rely upon the expert opinion of an individual in court as to whether the result of a match to a crime scene mark is valid, there are those technologies which are quantifiable, giving a numerical result. DNA, as we know, is one of these, but even these techniques are fallible. Police investigating a burglary found material at the scene of a crime. Using six loci to create a profile they then went on to compare the profile with the national database of named individuals. They found a match to a man living 200 miles (320 km) away, who had an alibi and also Parkinson's disease. The match was said to have a probability of 1 in 37 million of not being him. It was only when retested, at the insistence of the defendant's solicitor with a 10-point analysis, that the now incarcerated individual was excluded and released from prison. We need to be very careful if we are explaining statistics to a lay audience: 1 in 37 million does not mean only one person out of 37 million could have the same profile; it was also an error not to look at the other information carefully combining evidence.

Although it is not the aim of this chapter to give any information regarding the manner in which statistical calculations are carried out, it is the aim to give some idea as to the type of thinking and intricacies involved in probability. Statistical probabilities are the lynchpin of forensic analysis in court. The manner in which the data is collected, whether from chemical analysis, collision impact or a fingerprint, is irrelevant. The information which the court wants to know is made up of two parts. The first is whether there was some sort of a match between the data from the scene of the crime or accident with a known reference sample and the second is the probability of that match being found by chance alone. Sadly the second part of the question is often dismissed as irrelevant, as in the case of fingerprints where the unfounded assertion is made that every fingerprint is unique. There is also another part to the same question which revolves around error rates. In the case of DNA profiling, for example, extreme care is taken to avoid the possibility that one sample could contaminate another. Similarly, great lengths are taken to ensure that accidental contamination is not made by DNA from one of the laboratory workers getting into the system. Using this information it becomes possible to calculate probabilities of a match by chance and an incorrect result due to contamination or incorrectly analysed results. In the case of less rigorous systems it is important to realise that claiming infallibility is an inadequate defence for an error. The systems and mechanisms are in place to safeguard against these problems. If you have a clear understanding of the way in which your results have been calculated and the likelihood of their giving a false impression you will be able to defend them in court with confidence.

7

Ethical and Scientific Considerations for the Forensic Scientist

When a forensic scientist is asked to make an analysis of material, usually from a crime scene, the results will quite likely appear in court, which may or may not require the forensic scientist also to go to court to defend the results of the investigation or experiment upon which the written report has been based. There are two aspects to this which need to be addressed and although they may seem to be academic or theoretical questions, they are very real ones which need very real answers. On this basis you will need to ask at least two interesting questions: is this legal and right and is the science upon which my conclusions are based sound? When I say right in this context it does not mean scientifically correct, but morally right. Part of this stems from the not entirely correct belief that forensic science is always scientific. Some aspects of it definitely are, as they have been driven by science (DNA analysis is just such a case), but in some areas it is not particularly scientific at all, as in the case of marks left by tools and even fingerprints. I would, however, baulk at the extreme of the editorial in *Science*, 5 December 2003, p1625, by Donald Kennedy, which had the title 'Forensic Science: Oxymoron?'. Well at least that was a question. In an interview published in *New Scientist* in

Forensic Science in Court: The Role of the Expert Witness   Wilson Wall
© 2009 W. J. Wall

June 2003, Peter Neufeld, who was part of the legal team in the trial of O. J. Simpson (see box below) in the USA, said, 'Forensic science is nothing less than oxymoron.' At the other end of the scale are those forensic scientists who would claim that their arena of work is science like any other. Herein lies the problem and the solution, as well as a contradiction.

Simpson, Orenthal James

The case of O. J. Simpson has become notorious and not generally for good reasons. O. J. Simpson was a star of American football, which is why the case became so widely publicised. Around midnight of 12 June 1994 the ex-wife of Simpson, Nicole Brown, and her friend, Ronald Goldman, were found dead, stabbed, outside Nicole Brown's apartment. Simpson's children were sleeping upstairs at the time. The trial started on 25 January 1995 and lasted 134 days, all of which were televised. On 3 October 1995 the jury returned a verdict of not guilty. There was a great deal of forensic evidence which was discounted for various reasons, underlining the extreme care which should be used when handling or retrieving such evidence.

Not all investigations that are carried out under the umbrella term of forensic science are science; it just has the aura of being so and consequently carries more weight in court than it should. This is where the contradiction comes in and where ethical questions should arise in the mind of the forensic scientist. Generally speaking, those tests which are sound and reliable fall into the category of having come from an academic science background complete with peer review and can be demonstrated to be sound and robust in areas of work outside the forensic science arena. These sorts of tests include DNA profiling, which is used throughout biology and medicine, certain types of toxicological tests and chemical analyses, basically tests that have developed in medical situations where it is important to get the tests right to avoid killing the patient. Unfortunately some courts have been known to dismiss completely good, solid, forensic evidence for no good reason, instead taking up rather less scientific and less valid evidence, as in the case of Premananda (see box below).

Premananda, Swami

Broadly this was a state prosecution of an individual, Premananda, in the Indian state of Tamil Nadu.

Hearings of this seriousness are carried out in English, due to the diversity of languages in India, and also without a jury. This is mainly for the same reasons; there is a presiding judge who makes the final decision as to guilt or innocence.

The charges against Premananda were rape and murder, the murder being allegedly committed in April 1991 and in 1994 the arrest for murder and rape took place. The court hearing was held in the Sessions Court at Pudukottai, a small town in the south of the state. The disturbing aspects of this case are that, contrary to sections 330 and 331 of the Indian Penal Code, which forbids torture, there are several accounts of a level of brutality being used by the state which does constitute torture. Also the DNA profiling which was presented to the court as evidence was not carried out in the correct manner, the controls were poor and the results were not interpretable in the way that the prosecution claimed. This was, without doubt, the worst case of scientific 'sleight of hand' that I have ever seen. The only thing to be said about this sorry case is that it is now a human rights issue and the person carrying out the forensic analysis was not a forensic scientist, had no forensic background and was insufficiently diligent in what he did.

All this leaves us with a conundrum. Some forensic science is excellent, some less so, with subjectivity creeping into the analysis, as with finger-prints and hair analysis. In the latter technique it has been normal for nearly 100 years for this to be done using a microscope – a piece of equipment with all the scientific credentials needed to make the result also seem scientific, but it does not. In the USA several wrongful convictions have been overturned that were based substantially on traditional hair examinations when later examination of mitochondrial DNA was undertaken. Questions therefore have to be asked as to how ethical forensic science is and whether it should start making links and assumptions which society and the individual might not like.

One of the problems which forensic science does face is that a certain amount of the admissible evidence in court is accepted because of a rather clumsy circular argument which runs along the lines of 'I am a taxonomist and I know what an elephant is, therefore when I say this is an elephant, that is what it is'. With much of forensic science the wording would be 'I am a forensic scientist, therefore if I say there is a match, then there is one'. The trouble is that the taxonomist might not really know what an elephant is and the forensic scientist might not know the scientific basis of what they are saying, or even if there is any. If there is some doubt, then it should be declared. A great deal of what is seen as sound and basic in forensic science is fundamentally correct in a laboratory setting, but in the rough and tumble of a crime scene is far more difficult to assess. There will be times when you, or your superiors, have to make a call regarding the evidence, whether it is probative or not, and whether it affects the liberty of an individual or a group, as in the case of the 'Birmingham Six' (see box below). If there is any doubt then it should err on the side of the accused. This may sound strange, but the truth is that we should all work on the premise that nobody should need to prove themselves innocent. It is up to the accuser to prove an individual guilty. This can be a difficult and onerous task, but when carried out professionally gives a great service to the wronged individual and society.

Birmingham Six

This was an unusual case because forensic evidence was pivotal in the conviction and also the acquittal. On 21 November 1974 two large explosions took place in two central Birmingham public houses, almost simultaneously at about 10.25 in the evening. The devastation was considerable with 21 people killed and 182 people injured. This roused a nationwide search for the perpetrators, who were thought to be IRA terrorists.

The search came up with a group of Irishmen who were travelling to an IRA funeral in Ireland. As they were going to board the ferry to Ireland they were arrested. A chemical test for nitroglycerine was carried out on swabs from the hands of the men and returned a positive result. The resultant forensic report said that it was '99% certain that the men had handled explosives'. It is here that the problems occur. The forensic scientist had been asked whether the men had handled nitroglycerine; the forensic scientist had a chemical test for this – which proved positive. No other hypothesis was tested. There was a statistical anomaly in that what had happened was that the rejection of the null hypothesis at the 99% confidence level was inverted, but this was not important because the possibility that a positive result was found without contact was minimal.

The men claimed that as they had been playing cards on the train, the cellulose coating might have influenced the result. By the time of the successful appeal in 1991, it was shown that this particular test could produce a positive result from many different materials containing the glycerol/glycerine chemical base.

It is important to remember this point: the forensic scientist must look at alternative hypotheses, not just carry out a test and declare the results 'sound'. The chemical modification of glycerine to nitroglycerine is very simple, but it is not advisable to do this at home.

Before looking at ethical questions as general philosophical problems as they relate to specific questions in forensic science, it would be worth looking at some of the already hinted questions regarding the science in forensic science. Many scientists who have a training in specific subjects are often highly critical when knowledge is applied uncritically to forensic applications. In many cases there is a viable point, but where the real problems arise is with applications of empirical observations which then slowly evolve into a mainstream discipline which is part of forensic science. This latter aspect of forensic science has recently been addressed in a report by the National Research Council with the title *Strengthening Forensic Science in the United States: A Path Forward* (February 2009). It deals with many aspects of the organisation of forensic science services in the USA, which by virtue of its political structure tends to be done on a state-by-state basis, rather than being under the uniform control of a central body such as the Home Office in the UK. Among the other areas which were looked at were technical aspects of the science which was being used in court and this is of direct importance to forensic scientists everywhere. Starting with a quote from the National Research Council report we can look to see how this situation arose:

With the exception of nuclear DNA analysis, no forensic method has been rigorously shown to have the capacity to consistently, and with a high degree of certainty, demonstrate a connection between evidence and a specific individual or source.

This is a strong statement of doubt on the efficacy of forensic science, and so we need to look at the reasons for it and decide whether it is a correct interpretation of the situation and also whether it makes it unethical to take forensic results from such analyses into court. Part of the problem with the use of forensic science is the historical way in which it originated. You will notice that DNA analysis is singled out as having been rigorously tested before being used in court, and there was a large body of knowledge associated with variations found in DNA long before it found its way into court. Staying with the theme of personal identification, since this was one of the earliest areas in which forensic analysis was attempted we can see how the development of techniques we now take for granted arose with major questions unanswered about their accuracy and precision.

An early, no longer used system of identification was Bertillonage, after the inventor of the system, Alphonse Bertillon (1853–1914). He came from a scientific background with both his father and brother being statisticians and was appointed as Head of the Identification Bureau in Paris. It was while working there that he devised a staggeringly complicated system, Bertillonage, for identifying individuals. Bertillon also had another interest which was the analysis of handwriting and which resulted in a severe miscarriage of justice for Alfred Dreyfus. Although techniques of handwriting analysis have changed during the last century, as we shall see later, it is still of questionable value in the way in which it is used. In the case of Dreyfus, he suffered because testimony by Bertillon was accepted because it was from Bertillon, not because it was sound science with a testable pedigree. See Chapter 1 for more details of Bertillon and the Dreyfus case.

Although Bertillonage is no longer in use it does highlight the problem of unwavering acceptance of systems of which we should at least be a little wary, while reasonable scientific investigation of the claims of infallibility for some of the routine forensic tests are being carried out. Although doubt has been cast on the efficacy of a number of forensic systems, there is one which does cause some concern and is also one of the most long-established forensic tools – fingerprints.

Fingerprint investigation has a long history and the interest in fingerprints goes back further than that. The exact manner in which fingerprint patterns are inherited remains unknown. We do know that there is a genetic component from the medical use to which they can be put, for example several major genetic disorders so influence the overall pattern of the fingerprints that they can be used as a diagnostic tool on their own. On the other hand, identical twins who have identical DNA do not have identical fingerprints – they are very close, but they are separable. The earliest records of fingerprints being used did not involve any system of measurement or quantification, but referred to the Chinese, who used thumbprints to validate promissory notes. The method was simple: a thumbprint was made half on the note and half on the counter-foil, so only the note with the matching half thumbprint would be honoured as genuine.

Why have fingerprints?

Ever since fingerprints were first observed the question has been asked 'Why have we got fingerprints?' We know that there is immense variation in finger-prints and we also know that there is a basic set of features which can be used to define a fingerprint, such as loops, whorls, arches, trifurcations, islands and dots. What has never been obvious is exactly what they are for. Various suggestions have been made, such as for grip, but the features are so small that they could not significantly improve on the tightly held grasp of a hand. The reality is rather more interesting. The mechanoreceptors in the fingers, called Pacinian afferents, are extremely sensitive to high-frequency vibrations. These vibrations are generated by the scanning speed of the finger and the inter-ridge distance. Consequently it is possible to determine fine textures of less that 200 micrometres by running a finger over a surface. Even though the surface may be randomly textured, the finger will have a dominant frequency of vibration from the movement of the ridges which will define smooth or rough. So fingerprints aid in the perception of fine surface texture.

Fingerprints as a biological phenomenon were first described at a scientific meeting in 1823 by a Czech scientist, Johannes Purkinje. It was later, in 1870, that the first record appears of a crime being solved using fingerprint evidence. A Scottish physician, Henry Faulds, was working in Tokyo and purely out of curiosity had amassed a large collection of fingerprints. Knowing of his inter-est in fingerprints the authorities asked him to help in an investigation where a sooty fingerprint had been left behind by a criminal. Using fingerprints, Faulds managed to demonstrate that the man originally arrested for the crime was in-nocent, but, even better, when another man was arrested his fingerprints were shown to match the one at the crime scene. Although this was deemed satisfac-tory at the time, it was realised that if fingerprints were to come into common use a formal system of identification would have to be introduced. The foun-dations for this were laid down in 1892 with the publication of *Finger Prints*

(HMSO) by Sir Francis Galton. With the recognition of the value of this technique there came a realisation that a formal group of fingerprinters should be set up and so in 1902 the Metropolitan Police formed the Central Fingerprint Branch, which quickly started to amass a collection of prints so that by the end of the first year it had 1722 on its files. Most countries now have databases of fingerprints from arrested individuals and these will be clear and complete; the problems arise when the database is used to compare a set of fingerprints from a scene of crime with those which are already held on file. Prints taken from a crime scene are rarely complete or neatly left behind, but are usually partial and smudged. In recent times a number of questions have been raised about the use and interpretation of fingerprints in criminal investigations, which are worth examining further. Some of these questions have greater significance than others, but all will have to be addressed if the undoubted discriminatory power of fingerprint analysis is to be perpetuated.

The first question is whether a fingerprint is unique. It has long been held that fingerprints are unique to an individual, but this is probably only an assertion which can be made at any given time, that is in a temporal sense – yes, they may be unique. What we can say is that there is not an infinite variety of fingerprints possible. Infinity is a mathematical idea and should not be used as an alternative to 'a very large number'. Put another way, if all the atoms in the universe were arranged in every possible permutation there would not be an infinite variety of arrangements – the number would be incalculably large, but that is not the same as infinite. So even if we managed to detect a difference of a single atom in a fingerprint there would not be an infinite variety and consequently it cannot be ruled out absolutely that two people share the same fingerprint. It is for this reason alone that the calculation of a match probability should be investigated and the likelihood of a fingerprint at a crime scene matching by chance a fingerprint on a database should be quoted. Such calculations would be extremely complicated, but not impossible. The second area of fingerprint analysis which has been quoted in the past is that there is no error rate. This is a very unlikely situation because, as fingerprints become closer together in appearance, so the difficulty of separating them becomes more difficult for the analyst. Consequently there will be an error rate; very few things are infallible. It has been said in the past that if fingerprints were to be introduced now, they would not be accepted by courts without the match probability calculation and associated error rate.

It is the sense of infallibility which surrounds a lot of forensic evidence that causes problems in court. It is important to be aware that it has become increasingly commonplace for expert evidence from one side of a case to be contradicted by expert evidence from a different expert on the other. It is the historical context of this introduction of forensic science as a precise science, when there is no evidence that it is, that has caused such growing concern among lawyers and legislators in recent years. These two examples are not the only ones. There are calls for a far sounder scientific footing for such diverse areas as analysis of hair, fibres and paint to be looked at. It is interesting to note that while these established procedures are generally ignored when ethical considerations are being looked at, the legislature does tend to become more actively involved with applications of new and current techniques, proscribing areas into which science should not venture.

One of the more recent areas that has attracted legislation is the ethical and legal position of the human embryo and consequent children. Since the end of 2008 there has been the Human Fertilisation and Embryology Act 2008 which lays down areas of activity covering same-sex partnerships and their ability to receive assisted reproductive technology, as well as the production of 'saviour siblings' that have been screened before implantation for a known genetic disorder so that an already affected sibling could be treated by the use of umbilical chord stem cells from the second sibling. There is also the provision for the use of embryos that are human/animal mixes for research as long as the resultant material is destroyed after 14 days. All this is a laudable control on work which many people would still find repugnant, whether on moral, ethical or religious grounds. The point is that Parliament has legislated a framework on this so that the boundaries are set. No such undertaking has been attempted with forensic applications of science. Indeed, both Parliament and the Home Office have remained steadfastly silent upon this, even though it could be argued that the misuse of science in forensic applications could be seen as affecting more people than most other areas of scientific activity.

So if we accept that care should be exercised when dealing with untried science applied to forensic situations, just as other applied sciences have to be aware that their methods will be scrutinised, we should also keep in mind the moral and ethical basis of applications carried out in forensic science.

To understand the position of ethics with respect to forensic science and the manner in which it can help us to resolve questions regarding forensic applications, it is worth looking at what ethics can tell us in general terms regarding any theoretical enquiry. Broadly speaking. there are three sorts of questions that can be asked in ethics. They may seem to be very similar but can be broadly stated as:

- moral questions
- questions regarding opinions of moral ideas
- questions about the meanings of moral words.

To keep it simple, although there is a difference between morals and ethics, these terms can, with care, usually be used interchangeably. It is very easy to confuse moral questions with questions regarding moral opinion and in a traditionally philosophical sense these are not questions that ethics can answer. Ethics tries to answer the question of what is meant by moral terms and phrases. Although there is considerable variation in these between different schools of thought, they do remain fairly constant. So the first of our ideas, moral questions, can be as simple as 'Should I do that?' or 'Is that a correct action?' or even 'Is my friend a good person?' Answers to these sorts of questions can be either as absolute answers, which take the form of the individual's opinion at the time expressed as dogma, or as a calculated answer born of the values and ideas which are prevalent at the time. In practical terms the moral or ethical question 'is slavery wrong?' would have a different answer if it were asked of a twenty-first century Westerner or an eighteenth-century plantation owner. The social situation of the time influences completely the answer to the question, so it becomes impossible for ethical philosophy either to answer or even help to answer such questions without considering the social and political context of the time in which the question is asked.

The second question, which is a question of fact about people's moral ideas and which can be asked in the form of 'what do people think about slavery?', is, by implication, taking into account the social system in which the question arises. It is not the same as asking whether it is wrong, or what is meant in this context by 'wrong'. Slavery might be regarded as wrong, but the idea of the definition of slavery may vary from time to time and this will be influenced by the historical and social situation in which the questioner finds themselves.

In ethical and philosophical terms the third question is the one of particular significance. The first two questions are bounded by their context, the third question, when answered, should enable us to come to some conclusion. This is a rare situation because entrenched ideas rarely succumb to logical arguments except of the most robust and irrefutable type. In science, logical inferences are paramount and they can be used for settling ethical arguments. Just as ethical arguments can be made in many different ways, so there is a tendency for the moral ground upon which decisions are made in the name of ethics to be a product of society and what are sometimes referred to as opinion formers, whether these are the media or respected individuals. A logical argument is one based on valid inference, in which case logic becomes a theory of proof. The inference part of the description here is a process for passing from a belief in one or more statements, sometimes called a premise, to a belief in a further statement, the conclusion. If the original inference is sound, the conclusion either is guaranteed or has a significant probability of being true. In ethics the use of logic is laudable, but not always easy, as we shall see below. Logic works best in a physical sense, such as working out a counting system based on 10, rather than the Roman system which does not seem to have a particular base from which to work (but see box below), so every step in using the notation of I, II, III, IV, V, VI, VII, VIII, IX, X, ..., L, ..., C, ..., M to make calculations involves a new inference. It is awkward but possible to multiply and divide using this system, though it is not logical in our definition. When dealing with the vagaries of human motivation the problems are exacerbated because the same arguments will result in a different outcome with different individuals.

Roman additions

Although we have said that there is no particular logic to the mathematical notations used by the Romans, there is the vestige of a base 5 present, in contrast to our clear base 10 and a computer's binary base 2. This odd mixture of numbering can be used to add, multiply and divide, and of course it must have been since Roman commerce ruled much of Europe for several hundred years. So how was it done? By following a few simple rules it can be easily explained and there is no doubt that traders could do these calculations in their heads. The

(continued)

first thing to realise is that the number created by subtracting the previous digit is a medieval creation; the Romans would not have used IV for four, but IIII. Similarly nine would have been VIIII, not IX. The second important thing is that this is a calculation carried out without the need to see the way in which the result is arrived at – there is no requirement to understand the mathematical process, as long as the rules are followed.

So to add two numbers together using Roman numerals is simple. If we want to add 39 + 24 this would be XXXVIIII + XXIIII. If these are now put into symbol order we get XXXXXVIIIIIIII. This already gives us the answer, but if it is contracted it becomes more manageable:

Five Xs are reduced to L (50).

Five Is are now V.

The answer is now LVVIII.

Since two Vs equal one X, it is further shortened to LXIII, or 63.

This may seem complicated and positively perverse, but there are other systems which are even more complicated and illogical, but which when used from day to day were second nature and caused no real problems. Before the UK decimalised its currency in 1971 the system was pounds, shillings and pence. One pound was made up of 20 shillings, each shilling was 12 pence, so there were 240 pence (abbreviated to 240d.) in a pound. If an item was £5. 10s. 6d., that would be £5.52$\frac{1}{2}$p, decimal. Although it is not very logical in the traditional sense, following the rules of the system makes it as easy to use as the current method of commerce.

Attempts to describe the ethical and moral position of the individual in society have been with us since people began to think rather than simply act. Consequently, even if we go back a long way to see where forensic science belongs, the questions asked before forensic science was even thought of were still asked, but in a different context. Virtually any question that can be asked about the ethics of forensic science either has been asked or will be asked in the not too distant future as the techniques of analysis gradually get better and better. Some of these questions we cannot even think of yet, but they will be asked.

When we think of questions of ethics it is natural to look to philosophers and, more recently, ethicists, to help us make decisions of a moral or ethical nature. It would be true to say that questions of these types have not significantly changed over the centuries when they deal with the relationships between individuals within society. Where they have changed is with the relationship between individuals and society. Defining the concept of a society in this context is extremely difficult: we know what it is, but it is very difficult to explain. Perhaps the metaphor of a wave is rather useful here. We know what a wave on the sea is, we can point at it and declare it a wave, but there is no reductionist method which can define that specific wave: the exact same molecules of water will be in the next wave, but the waves are different, just as society is – same human beings, different society. So, setting aside the fraught problem of defining a society, what we can say is that while personal relationships have not changed much with time, the relationship between the individual and the state most certainly has, or, to put it another way, the reaction of society to its members is continuously changing.

We can see this change associated with the move from an agrarian society to a centrally governed industrial society. Sometimes phrases like 'post-industrial' are used to describe the economic base on which we operate, but this misrepresents the situation. We are still all industrial, we may be working in knowledge rather than manufacturing, but without manufacturing there would be no computers, no houses, no work, and we would have to revert to a pre-industrial age of being agrarian. With a centrally governed society it is no longer acceptable to exclaim, as Eudoxus did, that 'pleasure is the supreme good', because we are no longer individuals supplying all our needs for ourselves as individuals. Sometimes we have to be a little more altruistic than this for the benefit of society. Eudoxus (408–353 BC) was living in what was, essentially, an agrarian world in ancient Greece, where he was instrumental in the development of philosophy and geometry. Times have changed in the intervening millennia and we can no longer easily pursue the ideal of 'suit yourself' as we are far closer to being in a global ecosystem than ever before.

It would be true to say that for most of the ages where there has been an organised society, ethics has been directed, if not wholly controlled, by religious beliefs and motivations. These are very often laws, not ethics, directing behaviour on the whim of an individual, whether right or wrong. In breaking this mould there were several key thinkers, two of whom were Thomas Hobbes (1588–1679) and John Locke (1632–1704). Hobbes argued that when man is in a 'state of nature', that is effectively unregulated, uncoordinated and as a solitary individual, then the life of man is 'solitary, poor, nasty, brutish and short'. This quotation from *Leviathan*, published in 1651, sets in context the idea that we have to work together and think about our place in society, as well as who runs society. In the case of Hobbes his idea was that individuals should hand over control to a sovereign power which would control and guide individuals within society to the benefit of everyone. This may seem like handing control to a church system, and in many ways it was, but the movement was in the right direction, away from the blind following of a written dictum and towards an enlightened agreement with an organising individual, the sovereign, who can be replaced. It is only a short step from here to an elected parliament. It was Locke who formalised this idea in *Two Treatises On Civil Government* (1690) where he suggested that the social contract as described by Hobbes should be modified away from sovereign control and towards the idea that the social contract was there to reduce the absolute power of the monarch or parliament and increase the liberty of the individual. This has an impact on the ethical stance of members of society because, although they are under the guidance and, to some extent, the control of authority, they also have the free will to do things which are to the detriment of society, to contravene the ethical and moral state in which they live. Perhaps surprisingly, great thoughts and ideas in science can also resonate within ethics. For example, Isaac Newton (1642–1727) discovered laws of mechanics and developed mathematical expressions of these which could describe and predict natural events, as in the case of dropped keys: if you drop your keys they will hit the floor due to gravity every day of the week; gravity is not turned off at weekends. This rational reliability in nature – which was still seen as divine – meant that philosophers could look at ethical questions and try to create a system that was just as rational and reliable as Newton's physical laws. Later, in the nineteenth century, the advent of Charles Darwin also changed the way in which ethics was approached, applying evolutionary theory to societies, rather than species, leading to an idea that ethical and moral values were indeed subjective and born out of the society from which they originated. This idea of ethics was at least in part a subjective consequence of upbringing and society, but in modern thought there is a further development of this idea, propounded by Bertrand Russell (1872–1970). The change in thought is away from the individual as a protected automaton working for society and society working for the individual, to being individuals who participate completely in the life of society, being part of society. This means, of course, that some areas of activity by the individual must be kept in check for the benefit of others, but an otherwise unimpeded individual development is to the benefit of us all. There is in this area of philosophical and ethical thought the implicit belief in the need for personal development as this will make for a greater and more harmonious society. On these grounds it could be argued that in ethical questions different individuals will, or should, come to the same conclusion, although in practical terms this is not always possible.

Some philosophical statements do resonate down the years, regardless of the society from which they emanate. One such is from Lao Tzu, about 550 BC: 'One who exalts in the killing of men will never have his way in the empire.' This is peculiar because quite often murderers and bullies do seem to have their way in the empire (Pol Pot, Adolph Hitler, Stalin), but notice that their regimes are all fallen, built on hatred and distrust. What we want is a regime based on consideration for the individual within society and for other societies and systems of belief.

Just as these are laudable ideas, such general questions might not be up to the task at hand. They might not be applicable to very specific questions that might arise in forensic science; they may simply not be able to deal with questions that are of this time, questions that philosophers of the past had never dreamt of. One of these is the right to privacy: handing over personal data to the state assumes the existence of a benign republic and of this we cannot be certain. Even in countries that have a long history of genteel self-government, there are always episodes where we would not like the reigning regime to have data about us which could be used in an underhand manner against us or our family.

In the past it was possible to remain anonymous throughout life, if that was what was wanted. Record keeping was fragmentary in most parts of the world until the twentieth century. Think about it: everything had to be handwritten, copies also had to be handwritten. Going back to incunabula, there were no copies, everything was original. It was only with the introduction of carbon paper and typewriters that multiple copies could be produced; before then everything was handwritten and handwriting can often be identified. It took a long time before individual typewriters could be identified. Interestingly, the reason that computers retain the QWERTY keyboard is purely, and irritatingly, historical. It was developed for the typewriter as a method of slowing typing speed because, with a strictly alphabetical keyboard, it was easy to type fast enough to jam the keys together as there would not be time enough for one key to return before the next one collided with it. So we are stuck with out-of-date technology when there is a much better way of constructing a keyboard. It is now possible, within limits, to identify individual printers, but in most cases only while the ink cartridge has not been changed. So now it is not possible to remain anonymous throughout your life, unless you try very determinedly to do so. This is due to the amassing of data by all manner of people who really do not need to know it, like date of birth on a library card, banks, health records and forensic databases. On forensic databases data will be kept even if you are the victim – not too nice if you have been raped. There is really no need or reason for this other than the desire of the state to control individuals, so we come back to the idea that we need a benign state. There are difficulties in giving information to a third party, which is usually commercial, and that is simply misuse.

For the forensic scientist, data which is held has to be sacrosanct. It is no coincidence that court proceedings, although public and open, as they should be, can be closed to disclosure. It is not only possible but essential that a judge can defend the victims and the innocent from being named. Humiliation is never acceptable and neither is being embarrassed by being known for what has been done to you.

It is possible that there are only two arenas in which data is shared between individuals but never strays from the professional arena: forensic science and medical diagnostics. It is your duty never to do what is not right. This may seem to be an oxymoron, but it is very easy to fall into the culture where getting a result, of any kind, is enough. It is not – what you need to be aware of are the implications of your actions. This very delicate balance between forensic science and society can be clearly seen in the UK and other states which collect genetic data. All this has been officially sanctioned but is now being questioned as to the use, potential abuse and validity of collecting all this data. What we are talking about is DNA profiles being held on a database. First, a little background is in order.

As we have seen, a database is little more than a collection of data about, or of, a group of individuals or things. Generally speaking, nobody is going to object to the collection and characterisation of data which, for forensic uses, defines the chemical composition of, say, an explosive or paint. These are inanimate objects of no consequence in their own right, but the information does have potential value in the future; it will cause no harm to the product to store this information. But consider this: a DNA sample is taken from an individual, be it at a crime scene or from an arrested suspect. This is no inanimate object, this is the person who allows you to carry out your tasks as a forensic scientist and pays your salary. So the question remains: what is your ethical responsibility to the individual?

The UK DNA database is by far the largest in the world, containing as it does in excess of 4 million samples. Disquiet over the size and specifically the structure of the database has recently emerged with a survey of attitudes to the collection of data by the police and Home Office. The Home Office paid for the survey which was carried out by the Human Genetics Commission. The database contains samples from over 1 million individuals who were not charged with any offence and if they were, they were found not guilty. This includes 100,000 children. The imbalance among different groups was also seen as an area of concern with a hugely disproportionate percentage of ethnic minorities being represented on the database. Now this where it gets tricky: once on the database, the DNA profile stays there for ever, whether guilty or innocent. Even the victims, whether of physical assault or even rape, have lost the right to have their profile removed. These were the areas of greatest concern, along with lax security and no formal statement as to who should be allowed access to the information. The authorities currently controlling the database had simply not thought it through, but assumed that they were allowed to do anything they like, without any objections being allowed to interfere with the work. This is the ethical dilemma and by ignoring it they, the police and Home Office, have created a climate which is developing into one of distrust. This has been addressed by the European Court of Human Rights, which basically said that the UK database has gone too far in holding DNA profiles of people never charged or acquitted of charges. The problem rotates around the fact that although a DNA profile is a numerical representation of non-coding DNA, the cells from which it arose contains an astonishing amount of data about the physical appearance of the individual. If the UK government complies with this ruling then approximately 800,000 profiles will need to be removed. Retention of samples is a very definite problem because technology changes rapidly and what was once seen as an ethically indefensible position one year becomes commonplace when a regime changes and a benign government develops a rather less friendly attitude towards its citizenry. This is not so far fetched as it is now possible to use a system of DNA markers to predict defined simple eye colour, brown and blue, with a reliability of 91% and

93% respectively. For the composite colours the problem is still intractable, but high-speed analysis techniques will eventually yield the information for all eye colours.

Certain groups have to have the highest ethical standards which are rigorously maintained. In medical areas most records are now electronic and it is explicitly said that you do not look at medical records of friends, family or colleagues. The same approach should be taken for forensic material, which is where a big mistake was made by a forensic scientist in the USA. Ann Chamberlain was a forensic scientist in Michigan who suspected that her husband, Charles Gordon Jr, was having an affair. What she did was conduct an illicit DNA test on her husband's underwear – highly unethical. She did find traces of female DNA which did not belong to her, but that is not the point. It was unethical and after an internal investigation within the laboratory Chamberlain was fired for violations of departmental administrative policy. This is, of course, an extreme case, but issues of privacy are very important and should not be taken lightly. This question of illicit DNA testing is an example where the individual may not recognise the immorality of what is being done and since it is of little importance to the state it has been an area where government has legislated on an ethical issue. Generally around the world most, although by no means all, jurisdictions have made it a criminal offence to undertake a paternity test without the stated agreement of all parties concerned. By the nature of the process this is usually phrased as a secretive DNA test of an individual; in the UK it can result in a custodial sentence of up to three years and a fine.

While forensic scientists have a specific set of ethical issues to consider when they undertake their work, scientists in general also have ethical issues which they have to deal with. Broadly speaking, these can be covered by the word 'honesty', but within that there are two areas where this can undermine the whole belief in a scientific endeavour: the first is fraudulent science and the second is plagiarism. The problem with plagiarism in publication is that it depends on the scientific integrity of the individual not to do it, and the journal editor to spot it if presented with a paper that does contain plagiarised data. If it is discovered after publication it has the potential to shake any belief that the public have in science and the scientific method. Fraudulent data also has this potential, but it can be even worse in its result, not just in public perception, but also directly affecting the lives of individuals. An extreme example of this, though not, sadly, the only one by any means, is the misguided case of Lysenko and the way in which he subverted the idea of both Mendelian genetics in natural selection and evolution. This ruined genetics in the USSR, as it was then, for decades.

Lysenko and the misuse of science

Trofim Lysenko (1898–1976) was born in Karlovka in the Ukraine. He was educated at Kiev Agricultural Institute where he developed a theory of inheritance broadly influenced by Lamarck. He managed to develop good practices in horticulture among the Ukrainian peasants but took an unsubstantiated step further, where his political ability overtook his science. He suggested that heredity could be changed by good husbandry, affectively environmental inheritance. This was looked at favourably by the Marxist establishment because it was politically acceptable. Lysenko found great favour with Joseph Stalin and became the Director of the Institute of Genetics from 1940 until 1965. During this period it is generally thought that his theories at the very least compounded the massive famines of the USSR, advocating the planting of inappropriate crops which inevitably failed. So extreme were his views that he declared the laws of Mendelian inheritance to be incorrect and ruthlessly suppressed scientific opposition to his own teachings. After the death of Stalin in 1953 his star began to fade and with the rise of Khrushchev he became a spent force, finally being dismissed in 1965, although by this time the damage his failed mass agricultural experiments had done to the population of the USSR and the standing of Russian science was already complete.

Having looked at specifics with regard to forensic science, it might be useful, or not, to look at general issues which vex philosophers regarding ethical issues. The first such thing is trying to distinguish between an ethical stance and a moral one. There seems to be some confusion here in that in purely practical terms for a scientist of any discipline the two words are essentially interchangeable, while in philosophy they tend not to be. I say 'tend' here because frequently they are used almost interchangeably, though with subtle differences between them. For example, ethics is not concerned with the question 'is carrying a weapon wrong?', nor with the question 'does anybody think carrying a weapon is wrong?'. It is asking the question 'precisely what is one saying if one says carrying a weapon is wrong?' The first question 'is carrying a weapon wrong?' is, in fact, a moral question, although ethics may well have an influence upon the question. Generally morality refers to a code of conduct that determines right from wrong as defined by society; it can also refer to an ideal conduct which is agreed upon by society.

The position of ethics to morals is, in philosophical terms, the determination of moral boundaries, but for the forensic scientist there is one very important theoretical aspect of ethics which has a bearing on the law, especially arbitration.

It all hinges on the distinction between what people mean when they use a word such as 'right' and what they call using the same word 'right'. Take, for example, the moral reformer who can deny that capital punishment is right, while opponents say that capital punishment is right. They are both using the word in the same way and this demonstrates the difference between moral words, such as right, and words which define a function, such as colour. Taken to a (just about) logical conclusion we could suggest that two people who know all about an action, including all the details up to and including the outcome of the action, may still be in dispute as to whether the action was wrong. They must be using the word 'wrong' in exactly the same way otherwise they would have nothing to dispute. So there must be something else at work here and it can broadly be put as a moral difference, thus the meaning of the word does not, even in conjunction with other words and with what they both know, determine with any surety if the action was wrong. It is here that as an argument ethics cannot necessarily help. We can effectively say that both parties are right and the only solution is to try and balance the outcome between the two parties by arbitration. This may not always suite either party because it involves trading off various aspects of each position. Each side is right in their own position but if deadlock is to be avoided agreement has to be reached. Such black and white arguments rarely feature in arbitration cases that appear in court, simply because in the example above it would be most unlikely that there would be anything to trade between the two individuals except their individual moral stance. Should a forensic scientist be called to give expert evidence in a 'right versus right' situation, the moral and ethical stance must be that of a completely independent scientist, helping the court to understand what may be a very difficult and complicated situation.

In this respect care must be exercised when assessing the 'rightness' or 'wrongness' of actions taken in the past. Although it is almost universally agreed that killing an individual is not justifiable, unless, of course, sanctioned by the state as in times of war, or as a punishment, ethical problems, or problems with which we would now have a problem, were once acceptable actions. Take for example this passage written by Henry Mayhew in 1851 in his work *London Labour and the London Poor* (the passage refers to the 'river-finders' or 'dredgers' that worked the Thames in London):

> The dredgers are the men who find almost all the bodies of persons drowned. If there be a reward offered for the recovery of a body, numbers of dredgers will at once endeavour to obtain it, while if there were no reward, there is at least the inquest money to be had – besides other chances. What these chances are may be inferred from the well known fact, that no body recovered by dredgermen ever happens to have any money about it when brought ashore.

The implication here is that the corpse had its pockets checked for money, and presumably anything else of value. It would not have been an ethical dilemma for the dredgermen as looting from the dead already had a long history by the mid-nineteenth century. After all, the tombs of the Egyptian pharaohs were robbed not so very long after the deceased had been entombed. What was happening here was different: the person being robbed was newly dead, still recognisably a person, and it was not the tomb but the individual being looted. Even so, this was something that had been around for a considerable period; indeed, looting the corpses on the field of battle was supposedly one of the indicators of the end of the Age of Chivalry and so it carried on. If you were poor, as were the dredgers, then it was seen as a perfectly acceptable activity to make money wherever possible. There was no ethical consideration to be made, no moral point. This is why Mayhew refers to the observation without making a moral judgement. It would, no doubt, have been frowned upon by the upper echelons of contemporary society had they known about it, but it ill behoves us to make judgements from our position, ethical or moral, of a situation about which we have only a written word and never had to suffer the depredations of a group such as the dredgers ourselves. This is not to justify it, merely to point out that every age has a slowly moving perspective on ethical and moral values; we can only work within the ethical framework which is presented to us. For the forensic scientist this means scrupulous honesty – nothing else will do.

Appendix: Methods of Quoting Published Law Reports in Various Jurisdictions

When scientific journals are quoted the citation follows a simple system which is generally accepted throughout the world. With official law reports the method of describing them tends to follow broadly the same format between jurisdictions, but there are significant differences, which mainly come from the abbreviations for the law report in which it was published. A brief list, which is not exhaustive, can be found at the end of this appendix.

The points which are usually held in common in citations are:

Report title

Volume number

Page number

Year.

Forensic Science in Court: The Role of the Expert Witness Wilson Wall
© 2009 W. J. Wall

How a law report is cited in the UK

The first element in a citation is the name of the case, in the form of *A* v. *B*. This is then followed by the year in which it was reported put in square brackets, so we now have *A* v. *B* [nnnn]. Following this, there may be a volume number, then the abbreviation of the report type and the page upon which it is found. If for some reason a particular paragraph is required, this can be appended at the end in square brackets.

To take a real example, *R.* v. *Abadom* [1983] 1 WLR 126, this is the law report from the *Weekly Law Reports* of 1983, volume 1, page 126. It is not always true that there is only one citation for a case, so the above information could be also be found at *R.* v. *Abadom* [1983] 1 All ER 364. Here it is described in the *All England Law Reports*.

Abbreviations used in citations

AC	Appeal Cases
AllER	All England Law Reports
ChD	Chancery Division
EAT	Employment Appeals Tribunal
ECHR	European Court of Human Rights
FCR	Family Court Reports
HL	House of Lords
IRLR	Industrial Relations Law Reports
JP	Justice of the Peace Law Reports
KB	King's Bench
LRC	Law Reports of the Commonwealth
PC	Privy Council
QB	Queen's Bench
QBD	Queen's Bench Division
WR	Weekly Reports
WLR	Weekly Law Reports.

This is not an exhaustive list.

Glossary of Commonly Used Words and Phrases

Adjudication   This is the process of quickly coming to a decision regarding a dispute which is legally binding until any further legal clarification, perhaps in a court case, is made.

Adversarial   The process in law where the resolution of a dispute depends on each side arguing their case.

Advocate   An individual who speaks for another. In court this is normally a barrister.

Appellate   Taking notice of appeals. Consequently appellate courts are appeal courts.

Arbitration   A decision in a case made without the court. Arbitration can be ordered by the court or it can be mutually agreed to by the interested parties.

Arraign   Indict before a tribunal or court; to accuse formally.

Barrister   Lawyer allowed to perform the task of advocate for an individual or group in court. The complete title is barrister at law.

Chain of custody   The documentary proof which follows both documentary evidence and real evidence so that there can be no dispute regarding the validity of the evidence and its transit through the system.

Civil law   The law used in legal systems that are broadly based on modified Roman law, part legislation and part opinions handed down from legal

Forensic Science in Court: The Role of the Expert Witness   Wilson Wall
© 2009 W. J. Wall

scholars. It is also used to distinguish laws that deal with civil cases such as marriage and divorce rather than criminal cases.

Common law   The main body of law which is essentially unwritten, from the twelfth century onwards. It is supposed to reflect the common customs of the country in which it is used.

Court martial   A military tribunal for members of the armed services for serious offences under military law and some civilian offences carried out within the environment of the forces, for example assault of one soldier by another. Jurisdiction for more serious crimes defaults to the civilian authorities. Lesser offences are dealt with by a District Court Martial of three officers. A General Court Martial deals with more serious offences and is made up of five officers. The accused is represented by an officer known as a 'friend'. Field Court Martial proceedings may be made up of three or even two officers. Naval courts have between five and nine officers. No appeal is available to those found guilty. It should be noted that the plural of court martial is courts martial, very definitely not court martials.

CPS   The Crown Prosecution Service – the body which conducts most prosecutions (private prosecutions are the exception).

Crown Court   A court which tries more serious cases by jury.

Crown Prosecution Service   In the UK the Crown Prosecution Service (CPS) is the premier body which decides whether a particular case will be pursued through the courts.

Custodial   A sentence which involves prison.

Decision of law   These are arcane points of law on which the presiding judge has to make a decision. They are usually made using statues and relevant precedents.

Disclosure of evidence   This is letting the other party know what evidence you have which you are going to rely on in court.

District judge   A legally qualified individual who may sit as an individual magistrate.

Documentary evidence   Evidence that records the time, place or recorded statements that refer to the event in front of the court. These are such things as photographs, plans, recordings, etc.

Empanelled   Enrolled onto a jury or tribunal.

Evidence of fact   This is evidence which is indisputable, such as a broken leg or a discharged gun cartridge.

Evidence of opinion   This is evidence which is based on fact, but is an interpretation of the facts which may not be the only interpretation possible.

Examination-in-chief First questions asked of a witness, asked by the lawyer who requested the witness to attend court.

Forensic Used in courts and pertaining to the law.

Hearsay evidence This is something overheard, or something that someone has been told but not witnessed directly. Basically second-hand information. In a day-to-day example, 'a friend of mine knows someone who said that. . .'.

High court judge A judge who can sit in cases in jury trials, such as in the Crown Court or the High Court.

Indictment The formal accusation, a written document containing the charges against an individual or group.

Inquisitorial The process where disputes are resolved by direct investigation by an individual or tribunal.

Jury Twelve members of the public. These are picked from the list of those eligible and registered to vote. It is a legal duty to attend when summoned for jury service. There are groups that do not have to attend for jury service. Those associated with the administration of justice, clergy and those with learning disabilities cannot be summoned. Individuals who have been sentenced to life imprisonment, or any custodial term within the previous 10 years, are disqualified from jury service. It should be noted that for these individuals, it is a criminal offence for them to sit on a jury. For some groups it is possible to request to be excused. These are Members of Parliament, the armed forces, medical practitioners, those who have been on a jury within the last two years and those who can persuade the clerk of the court that there are genuine conscientious objections to jury service.

Locard's principle Every contact leaves a trace. When a crime is committed material will be transferred from the perpetrator to the victim, or the scene of the crime, and from the victim to the perpetrator and the scene of the crime.

Peritus Skilled or expert.

Precedent A quotable result from previous cases, thought to be well thought through.

Prima facie At first sight.

Private prosecution Sometimes the state, in the form of the Crown Prosecution Service, will decide not to proceed with a prosecution in a criminal trial. It is then possible for a private prosecution to take place. This is funded by an individual or organisation and carries the same sentences as a public prosecution.

Privilege   Privileged communications between a lawyer and client are private and cannot be revealed to a third party without the permission of the client to waive privilege; the lawyer cannot waive privilege. This extends to documents that are not going to be used in court, possibly due to their prejudicial nature.

Real evidence   Evidence of a specific and solid nature involved in the case before the court. This could be a knife, or a weapon of any sort, or a document with the defendant's signature on it.

Recorder   An individual who can sit in cases of jury trials held in the Crown Court.

Regina   The Queen, used as an abbreviation in court papers as *R*.

Rex   The King, used as an abbreviation in court papers as *R*.

Small Claims Court   A court associated with the County Court which deals specifically with relatively small sums of owed money.

Stipendiary magistrate   A single, legally qualified individual, often a district judge.

Summary trial   A criminal trial which is only heard in a Magistrates' Court.

Witness of fact   An individual who saw or heard something directly related to the case.

Index

Forensic Science in Court: The Role of the Expert Witness   Wilson Wall
© 2009 W. J. Wall

Printed in Great Britain
by Amazon